SEARCHING FOR ICHABOD

His Eighteenth-Century Diary Leads Me Home

BookSurge Publishing
Second Printing

Visit www.searchingforichabod.com or
www.amazon.com to order additional copies

Library of Congress Cataloging-in-Publication Data
Van Camp, Julie Foster
Searching for Ichabod:
His Eighteenth-Century Diary Leads Me Home /
Julie Foster Van Camp
Includes endnotes and bibliographical references

ISBN: 1-4392-2175-8
ISBN-13: 9781439221754
Library of Congress Control Number: 2008911564

1. Farming (Vermont, New York 1770-1813).
2. Foster family (1635-2005).
3. Genealogy.
4. New York history (Willink 1811-1813).
5. Religion (Vermont Baptist 1787-1811).
6. Revolutionary War (Vermont 1775-1783).
7. Vermont history (1770-1811).
8. War of 1812 (New York 1811-1813).

Cover design by Jonathan Dupuis

Printed in the United States of America

Permission to reproduce maps from *Building an American Pedigree: A Study in Genealogy* (Provo: Brigham Young University Press, 1974) by Norman Edgar Wright was granted by the author's widow, Daniele Wright.

SEARCHING FOR ICHABOD

His Eighteenth-Century Diary Leads Me Home

by

Julie Foster Van Camp

TO

my grandchildren
Ashley, Lindsey, & Megan Reader
Rachel & Morgan Van Camp
and
my uncle Warren Foster

&
Ichabod
wherever he may be

Genealogy is the study of world history on a totally personal basis. It is the study of exactly what role your ancestors played in the history of the world. Don't underestimate their contribution.

—Robert W. Marlin

TABLE OF CONTENTS

ILLUSTRATIONS

SUMMARY OF AUTHOR'S FOSTER GENEALOGY

Julie Foster
> Born January 6, 1937 in Cedar Rapids, Iowa
> Married March 30, 1959 to Robert Van Camp

Morgan Jacob Foster
> Born August 25, 1897 in Washington County, Iowa
> Married October 19, 1929 to Frances Hansen
> Died January 12, 1973 in Cedar Rapids, Iowa

Henry Lucas Foster
> Born August 19, 1858 in Medina County, Ohio
> Married September 17, 1885 to Hila Ann Jones
> Died November 11, 1919 in Iowa City, Iowa

Azariah Doane Foster
> Born May 10, 1811 in Whiting, Vermont
> Married December 13, 1835 to Martha Lucas
> Died September 7, 1889 in Washington County, Iowa

Albro Foster
> Born October 16, 1785 in Rutland, Vermont
> Married June 15, 1806 to Rispa Doane
> Died May 15, 1874 in North Eaton, Ohio

Ichabod Foster
> Born April 10, 1740 in Attleborough, Massachusetts
> Married June 5, 1768 to Susannah Carr
> Died January 1, 1813 in Willink, New York

Benjamin Foster

>Born April 17, 1714 in Attleborough, Massachusetts
>
>Married June 23, 1739 to Rachel Day
>
>Died January 6, 1803 in Clarendon, Vermont

John Foster

>Born November 15, 1680 in Salem, Massachusetts
>
>Married December 4, 1704 to Margaret Ware
>
>Died December 14, 1759 in Attleborough, Massachusetts

John Foster

>Born 1647 (baptized June 3, 1655) in Salem, Massachusetts
>
>Married March 18, 1671/72 to Mary Stuard
>
>Died June 1714 in Salem, Massachusetts

John Foster

>Born 1618 in England
>
>Married 1646/47 to Martha Tompkins
>
>Died November 16, 1687 in Salem, Massachusetts

ACKNOWLEDGMENTS

When I thought I could never finish this book, Joanne Foster of Virginia, a professional editor who happens to be married to my cousin Jim Foster, offered to help. She has single-handedly edited, nurtured, and stuck by me for four years. Without her, Ichabod would have remained buried.

I offer gratitude, praise, and deep thanks to the members (past and present) of my Lopez Island writing group: Emily Mallory, Ann Norman, Marion Spiedel, Danya Sterner, Roseamber Sumner, and Molly Swan-Sheeran. For many years, these women encouraged and pushed me to keep going, even when they grew tired of hearing about Ichabod. Other Lopez writers who read my copy and kept me on the right track were Lorrie Harrison, Phyllis Potter, Lorna Reese, and Alie Smaalders. Without my neighbor Dorothy Conway, and her constant encouragement, her astute questions, and her dedicated attention to detail, this story might still be sitting in my computer.

I am ever indebted to Foster relatives I did not know I had until my search for Ichabod began. Cynthia Meyerson of Oklahoma read my Internet message asking for information on Azariah, Albro, and Ichabod. She had inherited Ichabod's first diary, and she presented it to me in a brown paper bag when we met in Salt Lake City. Marge Goad of Oregon mailed me a copy of the second diary. The Cole brothers, Bill, Frank, and Richard of Kansas, made it possible for me to read the original second diary and guided me to the grave of Albro's youngest child, Ann Jeanette Hinckley, who had carried the diaries from Ohio to Kansas in 1880.

While searching for eleven generations of ancestors over the past thirty years, I uncovered additional living relatives who made me realize how deep our roots run. I value my connections to Judy Aversa, David Carr, Harrison and Holden Doane, Bruce Julseth, Eileen Maki, Pat Noble, Robyn Osborn, Pat Politsky, William Randall, Robert Sherman, Blanche Simmons, and Darlene Stone.

The following individuals and organizations offered me research advice, shared stories, endorsed my adventure, and welcomed me into their lives: Cherry Fletcher Bamberg, David Batterson, Alan Berolzheimer, Marcia Breece, Alice Brower, Sharon DeBartolo Carmack, John H. Conlin, J. Kevin Graffagnino, Hank Z Jones, Alan Manchester, Margaret Mayerat, Dan McKeen, Walter Phelps, Belle and George Senecal, Julanne Sharrow, Grace Simonds, Penelope Stratton, Gary Wentland; and volunteers and staff at the Family History Library in Salt Lake City; the Rhode Island Historical Society in Providence; the New England Historic Genealogical Society in Boston; the Henry Sheldon Museum in Middlebury, Vermont; the Vermont Historical Society in Barre; the Ann Story Chapter of the Daughters of the American Revolution in Rutland, Vermont; the Old Brutus Historical Society in Weedsport, New York; the Concord Historical Society in Springville, New York; the Reed Library at the State University of New York at Fredonia; and the Western New York Heritage Press in Cheektowaga, New York.

Thanks and love to all of you (and to those I may have missed). I am confident that Ichabod knows about all of you and is singing your praises, too.

Prologue

PROOF BEYOND A REASONABLE DOUBT

A washed-out sign leaning into a ditch informed me I was "Entering Whiting." I was driving north on Vermont Route 30. The year was 1992. Clapboard farmhouses and towering feed silos dotted the sprawling fields. The horizon burned in brilliant blotches of red and streaks of purple and pink, blending behind the black silhouette of the Adirondack Mountains. I passed a white colonial-style church with a cemetery behind it, several houses in need of paint, the town clerk's office, and a general store. Pastures, speckled with Holstein cows, spread across the broad valley.

Was this all there was to Whiting? I turned around in a farmer's driveway and retraced my route, looking harder for more evidence of the town. The afternoon light was fading. I had no motel reservations. In fact, I had not seen a motel since leaving Rutland. My fuel gauge was bumping on empty.

I came to a filling station offering grinders and gas, and pulled in. A middle-aged man, wearing bib overalls, a plaid shirt, and a cap advertising Hybrid Seed Corn, was resting against a stool behind the counter. He was thumbing through a magazine.

"Do I pay first, before I pump?" I asked.

"Sorry, lady. I haven't had any gas for three months. Not since water got in my tanks."

"Is there another station in town?"

"Nope. This is it. You might find one open in Middlebury."

"Which way is that?"

"About twelve miles over yonder. North."

"But I'm not going that way. Where might I find a place to sleep?"

He stood up. I watched his hazel eyes drift across the dirty windowpane. Chewing on the side of his mouth, twitching his thumb on the counter, he said, "Well, I hate to tell you, lady, but you're in the boonies. There ain't anything around here. But over east in Brandon, there's a nice inn. Don't know if you'll find gas there at this time of day, though."

He stared at his black, dust-covered rotary dial phone, as if wondering whether it was connected to anything. "Would you like me to call the inn, see if they have a room?" he asked.

Moments later he assured me that a bed and gas were waiting for me in Brandon. The scratchy weather forecast coming over his radio said we could expect another sunny April day tomorrow. I was warming up to Whiting.

"What you doing up here in these parts anyway?" he asked.

"Searching for ancestors," I said. "Ichabod Foster settled here in 1784."[1]

"So did my ancestors. Maybe we're related. I'm Guy," he said.

"Maybe so," I said. "My name is Julie. I believe Ichabod was my great-great-great-grandfather, and had a son born here in 1785 named Albro and a grandson named Azariah in 1811."

I told Guy that I had driven hundreds of miles over the past twenty years searching for my ancestors. I had tramped the ground where their logs became cabins and their clear cuts grew corn. I had rummaged through seventeenth-century land deeds in Salem, Massachusetts, marriage records in Coventry, Rhode Island, and probate abstracts in Taunton, Massachusetts. I had studied census data in Medina County, Ohio, and vital records on a German island in the North Sea, and fading photographs of Iowa relatives. Clutching my magnifying glass, deciphering tiny Old English script, I had followed clues.

"You're a travelin' woman," Guy said. "I pretty much stay right here in Whiting."

"Hope I see you tomorrow," I said. "I'll be visiting the town clerk in the morning."

Guy stood in the doorway as I walked to my car.

"Thanks for finding me a place to stay," I said.

I had trouble falling asleep that night. I don't know why. Images of people and places emerged like old sixteen-millimeter films, clicking, missing, refocusing. Almost visible. Almost hidden. I remembered traveling in our shiny blue LaSalle with my parents and my older brother, Jake, on Thanksgiving morning in 1946. I was nine years old. Our destination had been the Iowa homestead farm in Washington County. We passed Amish families in black, horse-drawn buggies, churning up dust along the gravel road. My father fretted about his clean windshield. Edging over to the culvert, he stopped, jumped out, and wiped it off with a rag he always kept in the glove compartment. After a quick pass over the hood, he slid back behind the wheel. Thanksgiving dinner was waiting.

The Foster family ritual seemed like Norman Rockwell material. Dinner was served at the "town house" in Wellman, after which we traveled the few miles to the farm purchased in 1860 by my great-grandfather, Azariah Foster. Aunt Mabel, her round face beaming, her apron a little off center, pushed open the swinging dining room door and placed a huge turkey platter on the table. The succulent, browned bird was a fresh kill from the feeder lot south of the barn. Uncle Ellery carved. The sideboards were crowded with bowls of creamed corn and scalloped oysters, mashed potatoes and brown gravy, tiny garden peas, coleslaw sprinkled with paprika, and cherry and orange Jell-O molds brimming with nuts and tiny marshmallows. Rhubarb, apple, pumpkin, and mincemeat pies filled a corner table.

We gathered to celebrate family, faith, and the fall harvest. My father and his four brothers, those five sons of Hila Ann Jones and Henry Lucas Foster, sat, legs crossed, on the living room sofas, methodically lighting, relighting, puffing away on their pipes and cigarettes. Aunt Laura refilled their coffee cups. Laughter filled the room as they relived childhood adventures on the seemingly endless Iowa prairie.

Nearly thirty years later, shortly after my father's death in 1973, I returned to Iowa from New England with my husband and three young children for one more Thanksgiving feast in Wellman. My father had been a pediatrician who diagnosed young patients with appendicitis but neglected the growing pain in his own stomach. He drifted into a cancer-induced coma and died shortly thereafter. Eight months before he died, my brother Jake had hooked a hose to the tailpipe of his car. The engine was idling. He pulled the hose inside. The windows were shut. When he didn't arrive home for dinner, his wife drove to his foreign car dealership and found him on the back seat. Bank records showed that he had delinquent loans.

When my father's ashes were placed in the crypt next to Jake's, I cast about for something to hold. My mother's hands were wrapped around her own pain. Her electric shock treatments and months in mental institutions during my childhood had maimed our fragile connection. We couldn't talk. I felt a cold, empty crevasse splitting open, swallowing me inside. I was falling without a rope, my spirit spinning out of control.

Knowing there was no one to hear me, I cried silently, trying still to be the perfect daughter.

Could re-creating my Thanksgiving memories fill the void I felt, help me feel the presence of my brother and my father once more on the farm, pass on a tradition to my young family? After our traditional feast, my children curled up on the living room floor. I sat on the nearby sofa sipping coffee with my Uncle Warren.

I asked him if we had any family history records, especially ones stating causes of death. The Foster Bible was destroyed in a farmhouse fire in 1923. As if on cue, he reached into his shirt pocket and handed me three small, tattered pages. He slipped his pipe from his lips. "Here, I think you should have these." His blue eyes twinkled as if they hid a family secret. He never said why he was carrying the notes that day.

The fragile pages listed only birth, marriage, and death dates for four generations. The notes were written around 1902, when my father was five years old. Albro, my great-great-grandfather, born October 16, 1785, in Rutland County, Vermont, was the last name mentioned. His parents weren't listed.

"Who were Albro's parents?" I asked. Uncle Warren didn't know. No clues remained. "Why me?" I asked. He smiled.

"Take good care of these notes" was all he said.

When I finally found time in the 1990s to focus my research, those five Foster farm boys were dead. I regret not caring when I should have, when I could have recorded firsthand accounts of life on the prairie, and asked my father what he felt when fire consumed the farmhouse or when he trotted his bay mare over the fresh snow to his one-room schoolhouse. These stories were silent.

But could I uncover other family stories among the records in towns like Rutland and Whiting, where Albro was born?

Would I find another Foster farm, a birth record, a death certificate? I had to try. My census research had shown me there was only one Foster family in the Rutland area in 1791 with a male child to match Albro's age range. I decided to seek the missing pieces that might prove beyond a census assumption that Albro was Ichabod's son.

Shortly after nine o'clock the next morning, I pulled up to the Whiting town clerk's office located next to Guy's station. A round-faced, middle-aged woman with deep blue eyes looked up from her desk behind the counter. "I'm Grace Simonds, the town clerk. Can I help you?" she asked.

"I'm looking for the birth record of my great-great-grandfather, Albro Foster," I said. "I believe he is the youngest son of Ichabod and Susannah Carr Foster."

"So you're looking for your relatives," she said. "Many people are these days. Are you a Foster? You must be the one who stopped at Guy's yesterday. A stranger isn't hard to spot in Whiting." Grace flew on autopilot without a verbal release button. Her energy, like a transfusion, breathed life into my travel-weary body. Her husband's family had lived in Whiting all their lives, and had started the Brandon Inn after the Revolutionary War.

Inside the small, one-story frame building was an L-shaped room with a counter separating Grace from the reception area. A room behind her cluttered desk was jammed with metal shelves containing volumes of dusty books. Moments later, she was lugging a stack of land deed records from the vault. Together we scanned grantor-grantee indexes in the first three volumes. Ichabod purchased and sold hundreds of acres of farmland between 1784 and 1805. Grace also produced a card file that had no record of Albro's birth or Ichabod's death. She opened a drawer containing a copy of an 1800 map of Whiting. Farmhouses appeared as black squares with the owners' names attached.

Grace stared at the map. "There's Ichabod Foster, right under that square. That farmhouse is still there, on the old Crown Point Road," she said.

I reached for the map, like a lifeline, a link to a family I thought was lost. The veins in my hands tingled. I couldn't utter a word. Was I going to walk across Ichabod's cornfields, sit in his parlor?

"My husband once lived in that house," Grace said. "Our families were here when Ichabod was. Ours didn't move on."

"Who lives there now?" I asked.

"George and Belle Senecal. They bought the house in 1944," Grace said. "It's been added to, but one of the original barns and the granary are still standing."

She made a copy of the map. I tucked it in my pocket as I thanked her for finding Ichabod's farmhouse.

I left Grace's office and drove down the dirt road heading west toward Lake Champlain. The Adirondack Mountains rose in the distance, reflecting the morning light, soft and pink. A few hundred yards ahead, a small white farmhouse came into view. My wheels ground to a stop. Gravel dust swirled around my windshield. Was this Ichabod's house? I couldn't move. I seemed to be entering a time warp, generations disappearing, coming together. My shirt stuck to my back as beads of sweat formed along my spine. I slid out of the seat and leaned against the wire fence edging the upper field. Grace's map assured me that this was the house.

I walked down the road, kicking pebbles, savoring this moment of discovery. Pastures of grass surrounded the small Cape Cod-style house. A small barn, shed, and chicken pen looked weathered and worn out. Weeds had replaced wheat in the fields. A robin pecked seed from the feeder hanging on an oak tree. Lace curtains lined the front windows. I climbed the cracked concrete steps and rapped on the door.

The door opened. A tall, solid-looking man with grayish-white hair and large blue eyes smiled at me.

"Lookin' for somethin'?" he asked.

"Not exactly." I paused. "Well, yes. Did Ichabod Foster once live here?"

"Yes. It's fact," he said. "He built this house a long time ago."

"I believe he was my great-great-great-grandfather," I said.

George invited me in. His wife, Belle, a short woman wearing a white embroidered apron over a blue flowered housedress, peered around the parlor door. Pausing a moment, she asked if I would like a cup of coffee. I stepped through the doorway, feeling as if I were walking back in time. My toes were touching floorboards that once bore the mark of Ichabod's boots.

We sipped instant Sanka as we walked through the house. Two upstairs bedrooms, a large living room, and an inside kitchen had been added since 1796. George pointed to the hand-hewn kitchen beams and wide wallboards.

The original steep steps leading to the children's loft were visible only from an upstairs closet. I pictured Ichabod sawing, pounding, planing each rough ladder-like step. They had been sealed off when wider stairs were added for easier access to an expanded sleeping area.

George wanted to show me the outbuildings. His dusty green tractor was parked in the old shed where Ichabod's wagon must have rested. I didn't know whether George drove the tractor anymore. His fields were full of weeds.

"The barn across the road is crammed with family paraphernalia, furniture and other stuff," he said, suggesting I wouldn't want to look inside. I did. But I didn't ask. I had hoped to spot some memento that might have belonged to Ichabod. Too many winter storms and spring floods had washed away any tools and oxen leathers left behind when he moved south to Middletown in 1805. Many other families had lived in this house. I thanked Belle and George for the chance to sit in Ichabod's parlor. Would I ever prove he was Albro's father?

I asked if there was a family cemetery in the back field. George said he didn't know of one but told me to walk around anyway. I found a little medicine bottle, a pile of rusty spring mattresses, and an old tractor rim. Nothing remained on the farm that belonged to Ichabod except perhaps his fingerprints on his kitchen beams. He had lived in Whiting, a town of 482 people when Vermont's first census, tabulated in 1791, revealed that Albro must have been a member of this Foster family. Grace had told me that 485 people and 2,000 milking cows resided in Whiting when the 1990 census was taken. This isolated community was ever changing, yet unchanged.

I departed with a roll of pictures in my camera and a handful of black earth stuffed into my jacket pocket, damp and warm against my thigh. Had Ichabod watched me walking through his cornfield, squeezing that clump of moist soil between my fingers? Had I found my potential link to Vermont history?

I had uncovered no clues about Ichabod's death or proof of Albro's birth. If I could prove Ichabod was Albro's father, my genealogical voyage would be charted back four more generations to Puritan Massachusetts in the time of the pilgrims. Was I a traveler trapped at the river's edge without a bridge in sight? The evidence I collected from land deeds, census records, and church minutes was all circumstantial. I had found Ichabod's farm, but nothing else. Did any other primary source materials exist? I felt sad when I flew home to my cabin on Lopez Island in Washington State without the proof I searched for, without a positive connection between Albro and Ichabod.

That evidence I longed for arrived unexpectedly five years later on a cool July evening. I was checking the Foster genealogy message board on the Internet, where I often posted requests to see if I could find living relatives. I was always disappointed when my request for information on Ichabod, Albro, and Azariah (Albro's only son) wasn't answered. Cyberspace had been silent for two years.

That evening, I opened an e-mail from a woman named Cynthia Meyerson in Oklahoma City. She hadn't seen my request before that evening when she decided to have one more look at the Foster message board before canceling her AOL membership. Why did she do that? On July 23, 1997, she replied to my request.

I am a direct descent of Albro Foster. Have part of a diary written by Ichabod Foster. Have the Doane Genealogy back to 1629. Know so much about Ichabod except where born and died, lose him after 1810. Some of the Fosters are in Jefferson Co. after 1810. . . . Is he with them? My gggrand mother Ann Jeanette Foster was born 1831 in Jefferson Co. NY. Albro and Rispa are living with Richard and Ann Foster Hinkley at the time of their deaths. Recently received copy of Albro's obit. I am thrilled to find you and most willing to share anything and everything. Hope you have info on Ichabod.[2]

"I have proof that Ichabod was Albro's father!" I shouted. I don't remember anyone in my family responding. I read and reread the message, letting each word penetrate my mind. I felt like a marathon runner who finally has reached the finish line. Albro was Cynthia's great-great-great-grandfather. She had the proof in Ichabod's handwriting. Albro's father had kept a diary with family records for his children, siblings, sisters, brothers, parents, and in-laws.

Cynthia's second e-mail arrived the next day:

I have been looking for Ichabod for over twenty years and I am overwhelmed to find you and that you have all this information!!! I haven't worked on the Foster line in years . . . really felt stuck. I was just fooling around last night when I checked the Foster names. You are the answer to my prayers. Ann Jeanette Foster and husband Richard C. Hinckley moved to Lincoln Co. Kansas about 1870. Ann Foster Hinckley died 19 Dec. 1927 in Lincoln Co. and my cousin Frank Cole still owns and farms the old home place. This family had lots of info but never did any research. My mother was given the diary in the 1950s and we visited Middletown, etc. on vacation when I was a girl. The diary that I have was one of a series. I have years 1785 to 1809. The others are lost. Each page is a month and is like a journal record.[3]

My newly discovered distant cousin and I clogged cyberspace for days, sharing and comparing family history records. Ichabod's granddaughter Ann Jeannette Foster Hinckley had carried the diary with her when she moved from Ridgeville, Ohio, to Beverly, Kansas, in 1880.

Cynthia and I met a month later at the Family History Library in Salt Lake City. She had red hair and green eyes. I have light-brown hair and blue eyes. Lots of gene pooling since Ichabod's day, I thought.

We sat at a desk in the library and carefully removed the diary from its brown paper wrapping. I felt as if I were unraveling a miniature mummy. Thin, hemp-like cord crisscrossed to form a laced binding that held the frail pages together. Edges crumbled. I could cup the diary in my palm. The heading on the first page read March 1785. The cover was missing. I have no idea in what year he started his diary. Ichabod recorded the events of each day in narrow, tiny rows across unlined pages, one page for each month. He missed only three days in twenty-two years. His penmanship remained steady and strong, flowing like a gentle stream across each page.

As I deciphered his Old English script, Ichabod's world opened before my eyes. He wrote about friends who spent the night; about harvesting his hay, making shoes, sighting wolves in the woods; planting cucumbers and corn, wheat and peas, beans, turnips, melons, even tobacco. He recorded the fields in which he planted them—the upper, the one behind the barn, the other east of the house.

11 April 1791
I took 15 sheep of Elijah Right to pasture and
he is to pay my town rate to Pliny Smith [4]

17 November 1793
We killed our hogs

12 August 1794
our earmark a half crop the underside of the right ear

20 September 1795
I see and eat a peace of ripe peach that grew in
Whiting it was 26 years ago that I see the last peach

Ichabod wrote about his treatments for various ailments. He cured piles with pine knots split and boiled in two gallons of water; he used beech bark, red nettles, strong vinegar, saltpeter, and mum gum powder to stop a bleeding cut. His entries were accented with tiny sketches of ships under sail, books of the Bible, birds in flight, fish swimming, flowers in bloom, toads, frogs, and peepers sounding off. Every spring he noted the return of the first robin. He tracked the wild geese going north. July was the month his spotted cow "took the bull." Weather was described: clear, squalls, fair and pleasant, heavy snow. Ichabod was a man connected to the cycles of life and his natural world.

He read the Bible from Genesis to Revelation at least four times. Each time he finished, he sketched a row of little books across the page, noting significant verses, such as Romans 8:20 ("For the creature was made subject to vanity, not willingly, but by reason of him who hath subjected the same in hope,") and 1 John 1:8 ("If we say that we have no sin, we deceive ourselves, and the truth is not in us,"). At the bottom of one page, he wrote "PROSTITUTION." Alone. In larger script. Was Ichabod concerned with sin? In one of his last entries, April 23, 1807, he wrote: "There are 1169 chapters in the Bible and to read them in 31 days you must read 34 1/2 chapters in a day."

I imagined Ichabod sitting at a small desk in his parlor, quill pen in hand, writing. As the sun fades, his wife, Susannah, lights a candle for him.

Where did he find paper, ink, and a pen in the wilds of Vermont years before statehood, during the unsettled times when Ethan Allen and the Green Mountain Boys roamed the countryside and soldiers marched along Crown Point Road? Land transactions recorded in Rutland show that Ichabod had traveled with his wife and baby, James Otis, from Coventry, Rhode Island, in 1770, two years after they were married. I wish his earlier writings had survived. The diary, with missing pages and no cover, starts in March 1785.

On the page for the month of October 1785: "in the early hours of the morning our son was born." The date was October 16. It matched Uncle Warren's faded notes. I couldn't lift my eyes off that line. I was holding proof beyond any reasonable doubt. Ichabod was Albro's father. I couldn't read the words anymore. My eyes had filled with tears of joy.

I sat in silence as I reached for a tissue. Cynthia smiled. "My daughters want you to have the diary," she said. "You are a Foster. I'm not, really. I'm adopted."

I looked into her green eyes full of giving. Did I care if she was adopted? How did she know I wasn't? I hugged her, wishing for words to witness my feelings. I couldn't speak or stop the tears from flowing. Was Ichabod watching this exchange, a twinkle in his eyes?

A few days after his sixty-eighth birthday, in 1808, he wrote his last entry. The diary ended. But his spirit kept nudging me. I didn't know what had happened to him. When did he die? Where is his grave? I longed to harvest the riches of my diary discovery, but suddenly my bounty wilted. Time stopped. There was nothing new to learn from Grace Simonds in Whiting. Where could I search next?

Ironically, my answer, again, arrived unexpectedly over the Internet. On January 12, 2001, I opened my e-mail to find a note from a woman I had never heard of. She wrote:

> Dear Julie:
> I am a great Aunt of Robyn Osborn [a cousin whom Cynthia Meyerson had mentioned]. I have another diary (or journal) written by Ephraim Doane. It isn't signed but that is the only conclusion I can come to. He writes about Ichabod on nearly every page. Some little comment—such as Ichabod left for Whiting today. Or Ichabod and Albro came by today. Also on the last page he has written—Susannah Foster died February—I think it says 24th—1820. Abigail Foster died December 21, 1814—37th year of age. Also Ichabod died January 1, 1813.
> On May 10, 1811—John and Albro had each of them a son born.
> I will send more notes from this diary if you want. It is very hard to read. Please let me know if you already have this diary.

*Or have no interest in it. Robyn has told me that you have the
Fosters done all the way back to England but I thought you might
be interested just the same. I know I always look for more and
more in the family history.*

Sincerely: Marjorie (Marge) Wiles Goad[5]

I felt confused and elated, emotions clashing, questions
bumping into each other. Something didn't sound right.
Ephraim Doane was a familiar name. He was Albro's father-
in-law. I wasn't trying to trace his line. I wasn't aware that he
had written a diary, and perhaps this was his second one. I
asked Marge to send the pages.

A week later a packet of diary pages arrived. I didn't wait
to reach my cabin to open it. I tore the wrapping on the road
as I stood by our country mailbox. The pages were larger than
those in Ichabod's diary, and were black and white, not the
patina color of his original. Clearly, it was a copy, but of what.
Who wrote it? There was no cover.

My eyes followed the writing on the first page. Suddenly
I couldn't get my breath, my cheeks tingled, but I must have
been smiling when I shouted "Hallelujah" to the blue January
sky. The neat, gentle penmanship was Ichabod's, and the page
started where Cynthia's diary left off. The last four years of his
life, described in his handwritten words nearly two hundred
years ago, rested in my hands. The Ichabod named in Marge's
e-mail was his namesake, his fifth son.

I felt as though I was holding a diploma awarded for years
of study and persistence, as though I'd passed the test given me
by Ichabod himself. When I returned to my cabin, I curled
up in a chair and started reading what he had written from
1809 to 1813. I held the final puzzle piece, the bridge across
the river. He recorded his family's final migration in 1811
from Whiting to old Willink in the Holland Purchase lands of

western New York near the shores of Lake Erie. The War of 1812 was rumbling on the horizon.

24 October 1811
We set out with our family & effects for the Holland Purchas

A psychic tug pulled my soul. Could I find Ichabod, feel his presence, discover his final resting place? Could I follow his trail to the end of his life?

Does a grave exist with his name on it? More than any kin I've uncovered in my family history travels, I am pulled to Ichabod, like a corn stalk stretching to touch the sun. Is it his name or the period of American history in which he lived? I can't explain the innate mystery, but a bond exists out there somewhere beyond the beyond.

During my 1992 New England trip, I had found his father Benjamin's gravestone in Clarendon, Vermont, and his grandfather John's in the Old Newell Burying Ground in Attleboro, Massachusetts, the town where Ichabod was born in 1740 [the town was spelled Attleborough then.]

When I located those grave markers, my crevasse of loneliness over the loss of my father and my brother began to melt. I don't know why. I accepted those feelings as a gift. I remember straining my eyes to read John's marker, trying to decipher the weathered dates and letters carved in granite. I sprayed the marker with shaving cream and wiped it with a towel, leaving the faint white indentation of letters and numbers. Sometimes legible, sometimes not, these stones, smoothed by rain, snow, and wind, confirmed the existence of these ancestors. Validated mine. My lifeline grew stronger.

In 1992, when I had driven from New England to the Midwest, I had found the stones of Ichabod's son Albro in the Fields Cemetery in North Ridgeville, Ohio, and his grandson Azariah in the Wassonville Cemetery in Washington County, Iowa. One grave remained a mystery. Where was Ichabod buried?

Could I follow my great-great-great-grandfather's footsteps and wagon wheels from his beginnings in Rhode Island to his middle years in Vermont and on to western New York where he died? Would my search lead to his grave? His travels covered a lifetime. My second journey to New England (the focus of this book) spans several weeks in October 2003.

I purchased my own grave plot before I returned that fall. I remember the cemetery grass squishing under my boots like a saturated sponge as I followed Dr. George Dengler up the slope behind the small country church on Lopez Island. A short, narrow man with thinning gray hair and friendly blue eyes, George handled plot sales. He pointed out my choices.

I picked one with a view. I'm not sure why. But it felt right. Cows were grazing on the far side of a sagging barbed wire fence, as their ancestors had done on Ichabod's farm. The distant snow-capped mountains on the Olympic Peninsula touched the blue sky, like the Adirondack Mountains viewed from Ichabod's fields.

A soft summer breeze brushed my face, as if confirming my choice, my contract with the earth, my connection with my ancestors, who had picked plots for centuries, honoring their parents, their spouses, and sometimes their children. Without their granite and marble stones scattered through-out New England and the Midwest, my family roots might have shriveled and died unnoticed, disappearing from view, remaining invisible. Picking my plot, anchoring myself to generations past, I felt connected.

As I drove home from the cemetery, I passed hayfields ready for harvest, sheep searching for shade, cows rubbing their necks on wire fences. I recalled my mother and her idea of a grave.

I laughed, remembering that she had never wanted family buried in the ground. Iowa winters were too cold, she would say. Her ashes, along with those of my father and my brother Jake, rest inside a mausoleum in Cedar Rapids, Iowa.

Could Ichabod have instigated my decision to settle on Lopez Island, to purchase a rural plot as my farming ancestors had, soil to shelter my soul for centuries? My family has crossed the continent, and so has Ichabod's diary.

I will return to New England to share his writings with Grace, George and Belle, and Guy. My journey will begin in Rhode Island, and I will trace Ichabod's 1770 route to Vermont, which he left in 1811 to cross New York to the Holland Purchase lands near the shores of Lake Erie.

When I reach old Willink, will Ichabod be waiting?

Chapter One

LAND WITHOUT A NAME

R ain peppers the roof, puncturing the silence in the Rhode Island Historical Society Library. Fluorescent lights hang overhead. I had flown from Seattle to Providence the day before to launch my search for Ichabod.

I slip my fingers inside a pair of white gloves, feeling as if I am preparing for surgery. Perhaps I am. I stare at a large manila envelope lying on a long table in the manuscripts department. The label reads, "John Lydius Indentures, Ichabod Foster." I slice the seal with a letter opener and slip his original property contract from inside. Karen, the department curator, points to Ichabod's signature. My fingers tremble. The sensations I experienced when I first touched his diary return. My eyes strain to read the tiny Old English script.

THIS INDENTURE, made the 29ᵗʰ Day of September, in the First Year of the Reign of Our Sovereign Lord GEORGE the Third by the Grace of God of Great Britain & KING & Anno Domini, One Thousand, Seven Hundred, and Sixty One; By and between Colonel John Henry Lydius, of the City and County of Albany, in the Province of New York of one Part and Ichabod Foster of Coventry in the County of Kent in the Colony of Rhode Island on the other Part, WITNESSETH, That the said John Henry Lydius, for, and in Consideration of the Sum of One Shilling Money, as also

*for the further Consideration of the Agreement and Covenants on
the Part of him the said Ichabod Foster, hereafter mentioned in this
Indenture, to be done and performed by the said Ichabod Foster,
he, the said John Henry Lydius, does by these Presents absolutely
Give, Grant, Bargain, Sell, Alien, Infeoff, Convey and Confirm
unto him the aforesaid Ichabod Foster, his Heirs and Assigns for
Ever, one Sixtieth Part of the Township No., Sisc, called Cambridge, Situate and being about thirty miles south Easterly from
Crown Point through part of the same Township runs Otter Creek
which Empties into Lake Champlain in North America Rounded
as follows (viz) beginning at a maple tree the South End Corner
of a Township Called Hanover hence Running west two miles &
forty Chains abutting on Hanover thence South thirteen Degrees
west Seven miles & forty chain thence south seventy five Degrees
East four miles & five chain thence North fifteen degree east three
miles & sixty-eight chain to the great falls in creek thence Extend-
ing the same course four miles & forty seven chain to the South line
of the township of Pomphret abutting Easterly on Fairfield thence
west two miles & fifty chain to a maple tree mark'd thence the
same course crossing the Creek to the first mentioned Rounds.———
Which Township contains a Quantity of thirty-six square Miles.*[1]

I wonder how anyone knew which maple tree to mark.
What happened if it blew down during a winter storm?

Most of the men from Rhode Island didn't settle on their
Lydius land. Some were able within a few years to sell their
undeveloped holdings, which had cost one shilling, at prices
as high as six pounds. Ichabod's younger brother Whitefield
did just that when he sold his holdings to Nathan Walker on
April 10, 1765.[2]

Karen, a slim woman with brown eyes and long brown
hair, leans over my shoulder. Whispering, as if to avoid
disturbing the document, she says, "Please keep those gloves

on. Oil from your hands will destroy the fragile paper." I rest the faded parchment page in my hands, grateful that the library is preserving proof of Ichabod's first property purchase. He was one of forty-five Rhode Island men who acquired part of twenty-three thousand acres of wild, unsettled land east of Lake Champlain along Otter Creek in what someday would become Vermont.

"How did John Lydius acquire so much land?" I ask.

"This is where the story gets interesting," Karen says, as she removes another indenture from the file.

She begins to read aloud.

This indenture was made the first day of February in the year of our Lord one thousand seven hundred and thirty-two between Carregohetego rujagararve Cannunay tar hard Egnite Canadagaie, the Chief of the Mohawk with their people living on Mohawk River, a branch of Hudson River on one part and John Henry Lydius of Albany in ye province of New York, Gentry, son of the Rev. and Mrs. John Lydius . . .[3]

Karen's voice is soft, confident as she pronounces the name of the Mohawk chief. This indenture includes nearly one million acres that today cover Rutland and Addison counties in Vermont. It was insignificant until after the French and Indian War ended in 1760. Lydius started to peddle generous leases for large lots among prospective settlers such as Ichabod and Whitefield, whose relatives, serving in the Rhode Island militia during the war, discovered this fertile valley along Otter Creek.

After the Treaty of Paris was signed in 1763, Canada and all of the North American territory east of the Mississippi were under British control. The year before Ichabod signed his indenture, George III became king of Great Britain, Ireland, and the 1.6 million colonists living in America. He was committed to taxing the colonies to pay for military protection and the costs of the French and Indian War.

The seeds of conflict with King George were planted six months before Ichabod signed his name in September 1761. The Writs of Assistance were general warrants allowing officials to search for smuggled material within any suspect's premises. James Otis was advocate-general when the legality of these warrants was attacked. He argued for five hours before the Superior Court of Massachusetts that the writs were unconstitutional.

By 1764, the force of the British government could be felt throughout the colonies. The Sugar Act placed taxes on sugar, wines, coffee, indigo, and other products imported directly to America. The Currency Act prohibited the colonies from issuing their own money. The Stamp Act taxed newspapers, almanacs, pamphlets, broadsides, legal documents, dice, and playing cards.

Ichabod and other colonists stopped buying British goods in protest. However, the day the Stamp Act was repealed, the Declaratory Act, which said that Parliament could make laws binding in the American colonies "in all cases whatsoever," was passed. One tax followed another. The Townshend Act in 1767 taxed glass, lead, paint, paper, and tea. In 1768, the year Ichabod married Susannah Carr of Exeter, the Massachusetts General Court sent a letter to legislators in the other colonies. It stated that Parliament had no right to tax the colonists without representation and asked for support. James Otis and John Adams had drafted the letter. Otis, whose father, James Otis Sr., served with Ichabod's grandfather, John Foster, in the Massachusetts legislature, is credited with the phrase "Taxation without Representation is Tyranny."[4]

Otis was "one of the most passionate and effective protectors of American rights during the 1760s . . ." In 1769, at the height of his popularity and influence, he infuriated a Boston customs house official with a vicious newspaper attack. The next day, when Otis entered a coffee house, the official beat him in the head.[5] He was mentally deranged after that and unable to serve effectively in the legislature.

That same year, Ichabod and Susannah named their firstborn child James Otis Foster. Perhaps the connection came through a political or family friendship that developed when Otis's father served in the Massachusetts legislature with Ichabod's grandfather.[6] In fact, John Foster, captain of the Attleboro militia during the French and Indian War, wrote a note to James Otis Sr. on March 10, 1748/9, asking for an extension on a loan. Otis had helped him establish his blacksmith shop.[7]

Ichabod was starting a family at the height of the crisis with Great Britain. Could the unsettling political climate have convinced him to move north to the wilderness along Otter Creek?

New York authorities soon issued a proclamation prohibiting settlement under Lydius titles and brought John Lydius to court on charges of trespassing on Crown lands under the province's jurisdiction. He lost in court and sailed for England in 1766 to press his claim and seek compensation for services to the Crown. He left behind some two thousand leases on his Vermont lands, and never returned.

Lydius had been an Indian trader and a man of questionable reputation. In the words of one Oneida sachem, who called him a "devil," he "takes Indians slyly by the blanket, one at a time, and when they are drunk, puts some money into their bosoms and persuades them to sign deeds of their lands."

Vermont was not Vermont in 1761 when Ichabod penned his name, not an X or a slash mark, at the bottom of his indenture for 380 acres of wild, wooded land bordering Otter Creek.

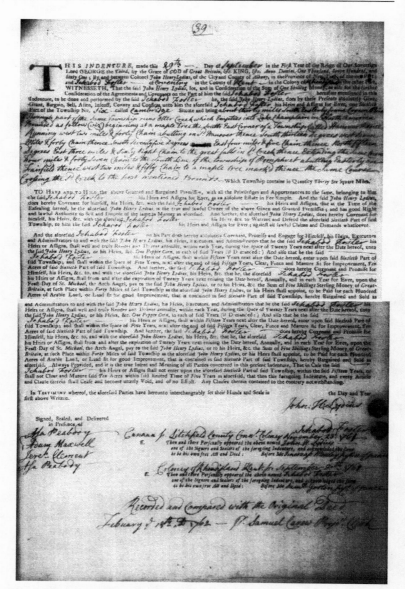

Ichabod's indenture signed by John Lydius on September 29, 1761

Lydius had mapped out thirty-five townships in his large tract, each comprising thirty-six square miles. He claimed to have received clear title to the former Indian land in 1744 from Governor William Shirley of Massachusetts.[8]

I picture Ichabod's calloused hands touching what I am touching. He rests his elbow on a rough-hewn pine table and picks up a quill pen. He trusts the unscrupulous land dealer. Ichabod hands John Lydius one shilling for his undivided one-sixth share of the township. The shilling had the purchasing power of less than five of today's dollars.[9]

I imagine those two men looking at each other: Lydius, age fifty-seven, slipping his shilling into his britches pocket; and twenty-one-year-old Ichabod rolling up his parchment. Little did he know that the Lydius land title would be worthless. I continue reading his original indenture with Karen.

Ichabod Foster . . . shall well and truly Render and Deliver annually, within each Year, during the space of Twenty Years next after the Date hereof, unto the said John Henry Lydius . . . One Pepper Corn in each of said Years (if Demanded:) And also that the said Ichabod Foster . . . shall within Fifteen years next after the Date hereof, enter upon said Sixtieth Part of said Township, and shall within the Space of Five Years, next, after the end of Said Fifteen Years, Clear, Fence and Manure it for Improvement, Ten Acres of said Sixtieth Part of said Township . . . from and after the expiration of Twenty Years, next ensuing the Date hereof, Annually, and in each Year for Ever, upon the Feast-Day of St. Michael, the Arch-Angel, pay to the said John Henry Lydius . . . the sum of Five Shillings, Sterling Money of Great Britain at such place within Forty Miles of said Township . . . Paid for each Hundred Acres of Arable Land, or Land fit for good Improvement, that is contained in said Sixtieth part of said Townships . . .[10]

The only actual settlement under a Lydius title was started in 1768, when Benjamin Spencer led the Foster brothers and a small group of others from Rhode Island to their township. They secured what they thought were legitimate land titles. The following year, Whitefield Foster and a Rhode Island neighbor named Daniel Marsh settled near Otter Creek in that part of Clarendon included in the New York grant of Socialborough. They worked together clearing the land the first year; the next year, they brought their families.[11] That same year, Ichabod purchased more land, a one-hundred-acre parcel located in Albany County.

I Elijah Osborne of Durham, Albany, Co., NY, laborer, for £4, 25 shillings sell to Ichabod Foster of Durham land in the township of Rutland 21 July 1770. [Witnesses were fellow original Lydius indenture signers, Benjamin Spencer and Thomas Green.][12]

Ichabod and his friends, who bought land from the colony of New York after John Lydius returned to England, experienced great difficulties. Their New York titles were challenged by New Hampshire and Ethan Allen and his Green Mountain Boys.[13] In 1773 and 1774, when the Fosters were settling their land, houses were burned, stock was stolen, and their town of Durham (as Clarendon was called by New Yorkers) was threatened with annihilation. Because Ichabod's surviving diary starts in March 1785, I have no idea whether the Foster property was destroyed.

Their neighbor Benjamin Spencer suffered under the wrath of Ethan Allen and his men. He was an active agent for the New York speculators in the Durham grants. The Green Mountain Boys supported the interests of the New Hampshire titleholders. A showdown occurred in the autumn of 1773, when a group of men led by Allen took Spencer into custody.

A judge found him guilty of "cuddling with the land jobbers of New York to prevent the claimants of the New Hampshire rights from holding their lands." The judge declared Spencer's house a nuisance and ordered it burned to the ground. I wonder if Ichabod and his young family crouched in the bushes, watching. In the end, only his roof was removed and replaced under a New Hampshire title.[14]

Title to the land was not settled until 1785. Ichabod had already moved further north to Whiting.

"Can you make a copy of the indenture for me?" I ask.

"Yes, but why do you want one?" Karen asks.

"This is original source material revealing his migration plans. I will treasure it. Save it for my children and grandchildren to read, as I have Ichabod's diary."

I tell Karen that I am tracing Ichabod's trail from Rhode Island to Vermont, and following the route he took to old Willink in western New York. In his diary he named all the towns he walked through and the families who gave him food and shelter.

I show Karen diary pages that I had copied.

2 November 1811
we drove to Wm Carr Herkimer

3 November 1811
we drove to Mr. Crouch   Skyler

4 November 1811
we drove to Mr. Clark's in Whitetown

"The part of his diary that was saved starts in March 1785, long after he left Rhode Island," I say. "I can only guess which route he took to reach Rutland."

I show Karen copies of two maps containing paths or narrow trails through Coventry and Bolton Notch to Hartford, Connecticut,[15] and along the side of the Connecticut River to the Crown Point Road.[16] "He could have connected with the old Post Road as far as Springfield, Massachusetts, where it turned east toward Boston," I say. "See the path continuing north along the east side of the Connecticut River, crossing at Brattleboro, Vermont?" If he had moved in winter, he could have traveled on the frozen Connecticut River to Black River and then on Otter Creek to his Clarendon land."

Karen opens a filing drawer and removes a map showing a trail twisting north through Rhode Island and Massachusetts. The route borders the Connecticut River in New Hampshire and crosses on the Crown Point Road leading west to the nameless wilderness.

"He could have left Rhode Island by either route," she says. "These were rough Indian and military trails."

Resting the trail maps next to my New England highway map, I mark the old roads over the new. I decide my route won't matter until I reach the New Hampshire and Vermont borders along the Connecticut River. The Fosters would have followed the river until they reached the Crown Point Road regardless of which trail they started on in Rhode Island.

"Have a safe journey," Karen says. "I wish I were going along. You're fortunate to follow your passion."

"I know. My flexible travel time is a gift of retirement."

I remove my gloves and lay them on the long table. I gaze at them, wondering if they possess Ichabod's fingerprints lifted from this original document with his signature. Karen hands me a copy, and then seals the original indenture in the envelope and carries it to the vault.

"If I uncover other information on Ichabod, I'll be in touch," she says, as we wind our way down the circular stairs to the main floor of the library.

"Thanks for opening a new window into Ichabod's life," I say.

The rain continues to pound the roof as I tuck my copy of Ichabod's indenture safely under my jacket. Questions crowd my mind. Will I stumble upon Ichabod's indentured land near Clarendon? Is it covered with dried corn or a shopping center? At the end of my journey, will I walk through his orchard in old Willink? Has someone preserved his grave? Karen is safeguarding his first property contract. Will I discover evidence of his last, bringing closure to my years of research?

⟨⟨⟩⟩

Sunlight laces through the white curtains lining the dining room windows of the inn where I'm staying north of Providence. The rain has stopped. A plump woman with black hair and a flowered apron serves me bran muffins, orange juice, and abundant refills of coffee. I am her only guest.

"Where are you headed today?" she asks.

"Rutland County, Vermont," I say. "From there I will trace the route followed by my great-great-great-grandfather to western New York in 1811."

"Why?" she asks. "Why did you leave your home in the West to take this long trip?"

I put down my coffee. She was not the first person to ask me that question.

"I need to connect with family I never knew I had," I say.

"But why?"

Words stick in my throat. How can I tell her about Jake and my father, untangling the tale of death, exposing my pain to a woman I had met only yesterday.

"If I can listen for the unspoken, hear the silence, feel the voices, the answer may come," I say.

Her eyes drift to the wall at the end of the dining room.

"I need to show you a picture of my great-grandfather," she says. "He and his brother came to this country from Italy around 1880. They built this house. They are buried three blocks from here. I bring flowers to them."

She lifts a small photograph off the wall and rests it on the table. It shows two gentlemen wearing suits and ties, standing erect on a large lawn, looking pleased. She carries the picture outside to the front porch. I follow her. She doesn't speak. The large lawn prominent in her great-grandfather's photograph is now a church parking lot. She clutches her treasure, cradling her memories.

"I'm struggling to pay off a second mortgage," she says. "I must save this house for my children, my grandchildren. Since my husband died, my income has nearly dried up."

Her eyes tear. Her hands shake. She, too, is a grandmother. Our ancestors, their legacies, their graves stir our raw emotions, creating an invisible bond between us. I touch her hand.

"Thank you for sharing your story," I say.

I walk slowly to my car. I am traveling alone, but I will not be lonely. She and Karen have left soft imprints on my spirit. As I follow Route 114, lined with vivid October colors, the yesterdays of my ancestors flash across the horizon of my mind. I imagine Ichabod dressed in buckskin knee-high britches and homespun shirt, riding his dapple mare through the Rhode Island woods. He had left his cabin in Coventry and ridden to Canaan, Connecticut, with his twenty-year-old brother, Whitefield, and forty-three other Vermont men to meet the infamous Indian trader from Albany and sign indentures promising to develop virgin land.

As I travel through the Rhode Island countryside to Coventry, I imagine him signing his name on the parchment, the paper I touched the day before, his wavy brown hair tousled, his blue eyes alert, his jaw and cheekbones, straight nose, and erect back giving the impression of a young man prepared to challenge the unknown. The pending adventure north permeates his young veins. I have no photographs or written accounts of his life before 1785, so Ichabod looks and lives as I imagine him.

He arrives home from Canaan. His indenture is rolled inside his saddlebag. My copy rests on the seat beside me. He notices smoke rising from his family's cabin chimney. The September air carries a chill.

After supper, Ichabod sits by the fire with his parents and his brothers and sisters. He shares his fears and excitement about moving to the wild land near Canada, the land of forests and swamps, of bears and wolves, the land without a name. His family will start over again, chopping trees, constructing cabins, organizing a church. His relatives and neighbors had fought the French in the virgin valley along Otter Creek three years earlier. They tramped across the fertile land east of Lake Champlain. Few white men lived there in 1761.

Dinner tables all over southern New England were enlivened by conversations about going to the territory that would someday be called Vermont. Fathers told families they were going, brothers tried to talk brothers into going, fiancées wept at the suggestion of going. The prospect of having their own farm was tempting when their area had become so crowded.[17]

I couldn't imagine cheap, unsettled land luring young families away from their established communities. However, it did. Perhaps King George's taxes were driving them away as well. Settlers such as the Fosters soon migrated north to stake out their lands buried under dense old-growth forests.

These first Vermont settlers, unlike those earlier ones in New England, "were all acclimated, hardy, accustomed from childhood to the use of ax and gun, eager and full of ambitious purpose to found homes and communities of their own," wrote Walter Crockett. "By a natural process of selection, only those fitted to battle with the wilderness, enlisted in this warfare. . . . As a rule the pioneers possessed good health and the power of thinking clearly and honestly. They feared God, and little else. They were ambitious, courageous and resourceful."[18]

According to Vermont historian Lewis D. Stillwell, Vermont was "one vast solemn, stubborn woodland that demanded dogged minds and hickory muscles for conquest. Vermonters were a climbing and creative stock, who delighted in obstacles, felt certain of their purposes and proceeded to make over by means both bold and dubious whatever environment they might encounter."[19]

Were these historians describing my ancestors? The Rhode Island Fosters were simple, strong people who trekked north with neighbors and extended family members, newborn babies and aging parents. Did Ichabod and his relatives travel in winter, when the Connecticut River was frozen, or in the summer following the path my map indicated to the junction with the Crown Point Road? Karen thought they would have traveled in the summer.

However, moving over the snow was easier. Most migration had to be done in winter, when the snow filled the hollows and covered the stumps of so-called "roads," when weeks of zero weather turned the Connecticut River and even Lake Champlain into smooth and solid boulevards of ice. A whole family with household goods could hardly be moved on horseback. The trails through the woods were practically impassable for wagons.[20]

Map of the United States in 1783

My route across Connecticut and north along U.S. 91 is clogged with road construction and traffic tie-ups, stop-lights, and eighteen-wheelers blasting their air horns. Lower New England is crowded with factories and freeways. When I am not locked in traffic, I push the gas pedal hard. I am eager to enter the north country. My past. My present. Would it be my future?

I turn east on Route 10, connect with Route 142, then 63 in New Hampshire. The gentle flow of the Connecticut River marks the meandering boundary between New Hampshire and Vermont. I follow the east side on Route 12A and cross the bridge at Fort Dummer, joining a section of the old Crown Point Road leading west to Rutland, the first road to cross the Green Mountains, the one along which Ichabod settled in Whiting.

Sunbeams flicker through the foliage on the eastern slopes of the mountains, highlighting a rainbow of leaves waving in the wind. Streams sing like songbirds. A truck loaded with hay approaches. No one is driving in my direction.

I imagine Ichabod and Susannah, traveling in the summer of 1770, the year the colonists in Rhode Island successfully protested the Townshend duties. All except the duty on tea were repealed. The British retained it as a matter of principle. Ichabod and his friends in Rhode Island, and colonists throughout New England, demonstrated their displeasure by drinking smuggled tea.[21]

Were they carrying smuggled tea with them to their indentured land? I envision them traveling with their ox-drawn wagon. Or perhaps they had only a horse. Ichabod walks. Susannah rides. Like women migrating north, she wears a wrinkled, homespun, beige muslin dress. Her brown hair is pulled back in a bun. Baby James Otis, born in Coventry the year before, cuddles against her breast, sucking. Another baby is turning over in her womb. She looks tired. If they had a two-wheeled wagon, it would have carried their meager possessions, perhaps a cradle, a few quilts, a kettle, a bag of flour, some garments in a small trunk. For the people who knew the grinding difficulty of clearing even an acre, the sight of the great Crown Point Road cutting for mile after mile through the dark forest must have been awe-inspiring.[22]

However, according to Luigi Castiglioni, an Italian nobleman traveling the Crown Point Road, "The tedium of that toilsome journey was increased by the gloom of the forest and by the disagreeable smell of the swamps."[23]

I wonder if some time during that year, before he moved, Ichabod had cleared an acre and built a small shelter to protect his growing family from wolves and winter weather. If only I could locate the earlier diary. When he married Susannah on June 5, 1768, his younger brother Whitefield and his wife, Lucy, were settled on their Lydius land in Socialborough. If Whitefield had helped Ichabod build a shelter the year before, it may have been a rude lean-to with only a blanket for a door, and a hole in the roof to permit the smoke to escape. Also, it could have been a small one-room cabin of unhewn logs, where the open space between the logs would have been filled with clay and mud, the roof and gable ends made of elm bark or rivet splints. Their floor was probably earthen. It was difficult to make a slip-log floor level. Shelters often leaked and smoked, and the wind whistled through the chinks between the logs.[24]

These Rhode Island pioneers soon realized their Lydius indentures were meaningless. Settlers arriving from New Hampshire and Massachusetts claimed the same land as those from Rhode Island. Ichabod and Susannah acquired the second title to their land through New York Governor John Earl of Dunsmore on April 3, 1771. Benjamin Spencer and his associates received "a large tract of land on Otter Creek lying Westward of the Height of Land called the green Mountains . . . 21,000 acres." Among the associates listed were Ichabod; his father, Benjamin; his brother Whitefield; and his brother-in-law, Gideon Walker. Their title read:

Land on both sides of Otter Creek in our province of New York. Part of the said tract within the County of Albany . . . beginning at a black Birch Tree standing in the South Bounds of

*a Tract of Land known by the Name of Socialborough formerly
marked Clarendon and now marked Durham . . . except and always reserved . . . all white or other sorts of pine trees fit for masts
of the growth of 24 inches in diameter for the Royal Navy . . .*[25]

How did Ichabod move these huge trees? Did the Royal
Navy drag them to Boston Harbor? His terms were similar to
those of his meaningless Lydius indenture. He had to settle on
his new land within three years and plant at least three of every
fifty acres of cultivatable land, or the grant would revert.[26]

New Hampshire did not honor the New York governor's
titles. Ichabod settled anyway. Land titles were rather loose.
Proprietors who owned large tracts of land usually had no in-
tention of becoming settlers. Actual settlers such as Ichabod
frequently "squatted" or "pitched" on land that suited their
taste without regard to the legal rights of absentee owners. Frequently no surveys were made. No clear titles were issued until
1785, the year Susannah gave birth to Albro, her ninth child,
my great-great-grandfather. The General Assembly of Vermont
(not yet a state) passed an act settling disputed titles that year.

Only adventurous, reckless people are likely to migrate into
an area where both the title to the land and the authority of
the government are being debated by armed men.[27] One Connecticut settler moved to Clarendon (where Ichabod's father
and brothers Whitefield and Joel lived) in 1780, the year British General Cornwallis surrendered to George Washington at
Yorktown, ending the fighting in the American Revolution. He
wrote, "vice predominant and irreligious almost epidemic. . . .
profanity debauchery drunkenness 'quarreling' by words and
blows and parting with broken heads and bloody noses . . ."[28]

Were these people friends of the Fosters? Were my ancestors part of this group that was "very litigious, quarrelsome,

intemperate, immoral, clownish and vulgar . . . fond of squabble and endless law suits"?[29] As late as 1789, a visitor commented that "the people have nothing to eat, to drink, to wear—all work, and yet the women quiet, serene, peaceable, contented, loving their husbands, their home, wanting never to return nor any dressy clothes . . . I think how strange!! Though they are, brawny their limbs . . . their young girls unpolished—and will bear work as well as mules. Leave doors unbarred. Sleep quietly amid fleas, bed bugs, dirt and rags."[30]

If Ichabod lived like this, his diary did not indicate it.

23 September 1790
Seventeen Baptised in the creek

25 October 1792
My wife quilted a bed quilt

28 February 1793
Church meeting in Wallingford

November 1795
I made Ichabod & Albro shoes

I turn west on Route 73, following a rocky stream, winding my way through the wooded mountains. Gray clouds play peek-a-boo with the sun, casting shadows through the forest. The rural landscape pulls me in. Suddenly my surroundings feel familiar, as if rising from another time. Vermont has never been my home—that I know of. Tingles, like tiny fireflies, scurry down my spine. Following the route through Brandon Gap, I arrive at the old mill town visited often by Ichabod.

5 May 1790
I went to Brandon

6 May 1790
Got home

10 May 1790
I went to Brandon

I had made reservations at the Brandon Inn—unlike eleven years earlier, when I was fortunate to have Guy call from Whiting on his rotary-dial phone to reserve a last-minute room. I sling my backpack over my shoulder and walk through the glass porch doors of the Dutch colonial structure. A fire is crackling. I smell coffee. A young blonde girl with a German accent asks how I spell my name. She pulls a card from a small box on the desk.

"You're on the third floor," she says. "You can walk up or take the slow elevator." She offers me an apple.

The first floor is spacious, painted in pastels, and divided into several sitting rooms, a game area, a pub, and a large dining room. I climb the stairs. My back aches after my long drive from the lodging house in Cranston. Did Ichabod have blisters on his heels after walking for weeks along a similar route? I feel tense and tired. Tomorrow I will search for the Revolutionary War fort south of Brandon, along Otter Creek, where Ichabod's father, Benjamin Sr., fired his musket at the British. I slip off my shoes and slide under the quilt.

Chapter Two

BACKWATERS OF THE REVOLUTION

When I walk into the lobby the next morning, I notice a man with thin white hair leaning on the reservation desk sipping coffee.

"Would you like a cup?" he asks.

"Thanks. Just black. No sugar."

"Where are you headed today?" he asks, sliding a steaming mug across the counter. "If you want, I can put you on the right track to the most colorful foliage around Brandon."

"Actually, I'm looking for Fort Mott," I say. "Can you guide me there?"

"What's Fort Mott?"

"A Revolutionary War fort south of here. My ancestors battled the British there on this very day in 1777."

"I wish I could help you, miss," he says. "Most visitors only inquire about our beautiful leaves."

"Do you know where Pittsford is?" I ask.

"Oh, that's on the way to Rutland on Route 7. Go south on that road across the Green," he says, pointing out the window. "Pittsford can pass you right by, so look carefully."

Moments later, I am driving back and forth over a five-mile stretch of Route 7 without seeing a sign or an old structure. Light rain slips down my windshield. I can't find Pittsford or the fort. I stop at a farmhouse and knock on the side porch door. A husky man with gray hair answers. His bib overalls smell of manure. Mud sticks to his black boots.

"Do you know if there is a marker for Fort Mott near here?" I ask.

He inhales deeply as he massages his cheeks. His eyes gaze over my shoulders.

"You know . . ." He pauses, wrinkling his forehead, "I think there is a marker on the road that says something about an old fort. I never hear folks talk about it, though."

I thank the farmer and start back toward Brandon. A few hundred yards from his farm, I see a stone marker hidden among bramble bushes. I park on the gravel siding and slip out of my car. The damp morning wraps around me like mist clinging to the sea. Crouched behind bushes like these, on this very hill, 226 years ago today, Ichabod's father, Benjamin Foster, loaded his musket. I glance at the sloping field below and try to imagine the dark forest of virgin birch and oak, maple and elm, sumac and ash as it might have been on the morning of October 17, 1777. The backdrop of burgundy highlighted the yellow and orange leaves. White pines towered overhead. A cool wind whispered of winter coming. But this day is remembered more for the surrender of General John Burgoyne to General Horatio Gates at Saratoga. Few remember the skirmish at Fort Mott.

Earlier that same year, those living in and near the Green Mountains declared themselves a free and independent republic. They wrote their own constitution, coined their own money, outlawed slavery, and kept out invaders, including New Yorkers. They even considered uniting with Canada. This independent state of Vermont built the fort that Benjamin set out to defend. The marker I find near the road mentions only Fort Vengeance, one built above Fort Mott in 1779.

I walk down the hill through dried stalks of corn, a witness to my family history. American history becomes my history.

At this moment, Pittsford is the most significant battle of the war. I want people to know how brave these men had been. Pride is captured in my lens of history, filtered through time, enlarged, zoomed in, focusing on my slice of the Revolutionary War. I imagine the sounds of musket fire erupting from behind crusty tree trunks along the deer trail, the only land route between Clarendon and Pittsford. A tall line of hemlock logs had been set lengthwise in the ground surrounding a square structure. The deck on Fort Mott was designed to collect fresh water for the settlers and militia inside. I see no sign of the fort.

My mind meanders back to my high school history class when I memorized dates like April 19, 1775. We had studied generals named Gates and Washington, Burgoyne and Cornwallis, and places called Yorktown, Saratoga, and Bunker Hill, where famous battles occurred. I don't remember any teachers mentioning Brandon or Pittsford, Fort Mott or Hubbardton, the places where my family fought. The Fosters had settled on the fringe, fighting for the northernmost lands of liberty. They had no uniforms. They were farmers who volunteered to protect each other. They were the local militia.

I wonder what these farmers looked like as they slipped through the underbrush that day. In his diary, a German Hessian mercenary described the dress of Benjamin and other Vermont militia.

They wore small clothes, coming down and fastening just below the knee, and long stockings with cowhide shoes ornamented by large buckles while not a pair of boots graced the company. The coats and waist coats were loose and of huge dimensions, with colors as various as the barks of oak, sumac and other trees. Their shirts were all made of flax and, like every other part of the dress, were homespun. On their heads was worn a large round-top and broad-brimmed hat.[1]

There were no homespun outfits for the mercenaries. They dressed in matching red uniforms, making them all the easier for Benjamin to pick off from his position behind a maple tree.

I continue walking through the field where he had joined Captain Abraham Salisbury's company along Otter Creek. They had dropped their scythes, abandoned the reins of their yoked oxen, and run to round up their neighbors. They raced north through the forest or paddled canoes down Otter Creek. These farmers became militiamen in minutes, answering the call to protect the thirty-five families living in Pittsford from Tories, Indians, Hessian, and British soldiers, who had been plundering and raiding the town, carrying off young children as prisoners. In late September 1777, Indians had seized two young boys from Pittsford, Joseph and John Rowley, and taken them to Canada. Two days later, Indians captured two more boys. Felix Powell's house was attacked that night. Mr. Powell was not home. Mrs. Powell, believing an attack was imminent, had fled into a thick cluster of bushes. While she watched her house burn, she gave birth to a baby.[2]

Word of the plight of Pittsford spread south. That was when the Clarendon farmers joined the call to attempt to recover the children and to protect the inhabitants. Why did Ichabod not answer Captain Salisbury's call? His father, Benjamin, did at age sixty-three. Ichabod was his oldest child. Maybe he had taken his young family to safety in Massachusetts or back to Rhode Island. His first child, James Otis, who traveled in his mother's arms from Coventry, had died ten months before during a dysentery outbreak in the Clarendon area. He and Susannah had four other children by then, and she was three months pregnant with another.

The problems for Pittsford settlers began several months before the Rowley brothers were captured. The British had planned massive military operations for the northern region that year.[3] Under General Burgoyne, a professional soldier, playwright, and politician, a glittering entourage officially known as the Northern British Army started up Lake Champlain from Canada in June. Bands played. Banners fluttered. Dressed in scarlet and green, white and blue uniforms, 4,135 British, 3,116 German (Hessian), and 148 Canadian soldiers were supported by more than 500 Indians.[4]

Burgoyne had practically promised "to cross America in a hop, step and a jump."[5] Instead, the playboy general had to cut through the forests, making his way down the Hudson Valley, while being harassed by the militia. Ichabod's family and neighbors were among those insurgents who diverted streams, felled trees, and destroyed bridges, making Burgoyne's wild terrain even more impassable. His entourage was more than three miles long, and his personal baggage took up more than thirty carts.[6]

Fort Ticonderoga, which Ethan Allen and his Green Mountain Boys had captured without a shot fired in 1775, was still controlled by the Patriots. General Arthur St. Clair, with only 2,540 militia, knew he was greatly outnumbered by General Burgoyne. He gave orders to evacuate the fort. Benjamin Jr., one of Ichabod's younger brothers, was among the ranks.

They left Fort Ticonderoga on July 6 and retreated to Castleton. Now that the fort was abandoned, the entire Otter Creek valley lay open to attack from the north and west. Gloom, heavier than the July heat, hung over the scattered clearings.[7] Seth Warner's rear guard of three regiments was badly beaten in the Battle of Hubbardton, west of Fort Mott, the next day. People in Pittsford left their homes and hid in the woods, expecting the enemy to attack. Many fled in fear, south to Clarendon, where the Fosters lived.

Their fear was justified. Within twenty-four hours, Hessians, Tories, and Indians rendered the whole area around Brandon and Pittsford an almost empty wasteland, devoid of people and domestic animals. Buildings and crops were burned. No other section of Vermont and few regions of New England were so hard hit or suffered more throughout the Revolution than this countryside along Otter Creek.[8]

During the panic that followed the retreat from Fort Ticonderoga, Benjamin Jr. was taken prisoner. He was placed under the guard of Hessians at Skenesborough (White Hall) on Lake Champlain three months before his father, Benjamin, joined the militia to protect Fort Mott. He escaped two weeks later.[9]

I picture him, ragged and hungry, slipping away from the German mercenaries, sneaking through the woods past Fort Mott back to Clarendon, following the deer trail along Otter Creek. Benjamin Jr. was the first Foster to enter the Vermont militia, enlisting with Captain Thomas Sawyer in the spring of 1777. He worked on the Crown Point Road from Charlestown in New Hampshire to Ticonderoga, which was used to transport artillery and military. He helped construct the Clarendon blockhouse, where inhabitants hid during frequent raids, and he continued with the militia until the end of the war. During that period, he built forts; fortified garrisons; hauled military stores; and rounded up abandoned cattle, sheep, pigs, and other livestock and herded them to safety in the Berkshires.

On his return from one of these trips to Massachusetts, he was ordered to oppose a party sent out by General Burgoyne to destroy military stores. Patriots had gathered cattle, horses, and shell carriages about twenty miles east of the Hudson River at the obscure village of Bennington. The Continentals and the militia under the command of General John Stark defeated the British and the Hessians on August 16, 1777, the day before Benjamin arrived.

He continued to serve as a corporal and a sergeant on excursions against the Tories and the Indians until General Burgoyne surrendered at Saratoga two months later, on the same day his father, Benjamin, joined the militia. That defeat changed the course of the war. The British Parliament resisted sending more arms to America, and the French became more interested in an alliance with the colonists that would avenge its defeat by the British in the Seven Years' War.[10]

General Burgoyne did not speak kindly of the Fosters and their fellow militia following his defeat at Saratoga. "This country [Vermont] abounds in the most active and most rebellious race of the continent, and hangs like a gathering storm upon my left."[11]

I stand in the grass looking at the fields where my relatives fought for their families, for their lives, living in fear of Indians and Tories ready to kill them with musket fire or stab them in the neck around the next bend. I have never felt the fear of war firsthand. I'm awestruck. My ancestors lived with it, survived in it, for six years. The war ended with the surrender of General Cornwallis at Yorktown on October 17, 1781, four years to the day after the call came to protect Pittsford.

Sunlight struggles to show its face. I return to my car, turn south on Route 7, and drive through Rutland to the small Marsh family cemetery located on the west side of Middle Road a few miles north of the Clarendon Town Hall. Ichabod's father, Benjamin, is buried here. (Benjamin Jr. is buried in Sharon Township, Medina County, Ohio.)

Brown slippery leaves stick together, clinging to my boots as I squeeze under the padlocked chain between the fence post and the gate. The south and west parts contain old markers. Oak trees, their leaves lost to another season, line the sagging fence. Bushes snake along the edges, reclaiming their space from the past, before settlers arrived. The lumpy middle section has no visible markers. I walk toward Benjamin's grave on the west side, where I had found it during my first visit to Vermont in 1992. The Foster double stone, honoring Benjamin and his son Whitefield, is surrounded by two centuries of Marsh graves.

I rub my fingers across the rough surface and try to picture the Marshes and the Fosters together cutting trees before this land was a family burial ground. They were Otter Creek neighbors who signed indentures with John Lydius in 1761, and were among the first pioneers to reach out beyond the original thirteen colonies to clear forests, build cabins, and plant corn for the first time on this virgin land.

I look beyond the fence, across the flat farmland, and see in the distance the same creek that flowed through this rich valley when their ancestors battled the French and the Indians in 1759, the creek that drew these Rhode Island settlers to the north country without a name. Is this the land these two families purchased in 1761 for a peppercorn per year? The creek and the mountains beyond define the western border named in their indentures. I want to kiss the ground and claim it as mine. Something inside, unnamed, whispers to me, "You are right." Or is the whisper just a wish?

Several years after the Fosters and the Marshes signed their land contracts, they traveled from Rhode Island and, side by side, chopped trees and layered logs for each other's cabins.[12] Were Daniel Marsh and Benjamin Foster Sr. cutting cornstalks together on this land along Otter Creek that October morning when the alarm was heard to march to Pittsford? Daniel did not answer. Benjamin did.

With the defeat of the British forces at Saratoga, those like Daniel were objects of patriot vengeance. On March 26, 1778, the governor and council, through the authority of the Vermont General Assembly (a free republic), appointed a court of confiscation to order the sale of estates both real and personal belonging to the enemies of the United States:

. . . having maturely considered the several proofs that were exhibited . . . therein have by the notorious treasonable acts committed against this and the United States of America forfeited the whole of their real and personal estate . . . and the money arising from such sales . . . be put into the public treasury of this state . . .[13]

Sixteen former Clarendon residents fell under this act. Daniel's farmland had been confiscated and his citizenship in Vermont removed. He was a Tory who fled to Connecticut during the war. Those who had left the state were forbidden to return. If they did, they received between twenty and fifty lashes on a naked back. A second violation resulted in death. Daniel Marsh was one who survived. He contested the seizure of his property and attempted to restore his public trust. The town voted to receive him as "a good, wholesome inhabitant" on December 16, 1782.

An Act Enabling Daniel Marsh Late a Prisoner, Taken by American Troops from Within the Enemy's Lines, to Return to his farm in Clarendon, and take peaceable possession thereof . . . that said Daniel Marsh shall be, and he is hereby declared to be, restored to the Possession of his Property and to all the Privileges of a Subject of this state . . .[14]

This petition stated:
. . . being one of the first planters of the town of Clarendon, and undergoing all the fatigues and hardships of a New beginner

in a wilderness & having for some time been Deprived the privilege of Enjoying the title your petitioner acquir'd by long & painful Industry Humbly Prays for Liberty from the Honorable House to be Restor'd to his former Privileges to Remain a peaceable & faithful Subject of the State of Vermont . . .[15]

While he was away, one Silas Whitney occupied his farm. Marsh carried on a running battle for several years in the courts and on the land itself to regain title to his property. During the struggle, one party would sow and the other would reap, one would install a tenant and the other would evict him. On one occasion, Whitney mowed several acres of hay on a disputed meadow, and while he was eating dinner, Marsh, with the assistance of others, drew it all away.[16] Were the Fosters among those "assisting"?

Others with family connections whose land had been confiscated were Daniel Walker, father of patriot Ensign Gideon Walker, who was married to Ichabod's sister, Rachel, and Elijah Osbourn, from whom Ichabod purchased his first piece of property outright in 1770.

Family fences were mended. Today, the bodies of Daniel and Benjamin rest in this same small Clarendon cemetery on property that was restored to the Marsh family. Sixty-nine graves are listed in the cemetery record book, many now without markers.

Daniel's stone reads:

Daniel Marsh, Esq
who in the 60th year of his age
with an unshaken belief
of a blessed immortality and final restoration of all things
calmly departed his life
Feb 29, 1808

Ironically, even though the property of this Tory had been confiscated on April 23, 1778, I notice his grave has a Sons of the Revolution marker beside it.

Apparently, he successfully petitioned the General Assembly to consider his service of sixteen days in providing hay, horses, and transportation to Montreal for Captain Oliver Potter's company during the Canadian Expedition of 1775. This service occurred before his alleged Tory activities.[17]

Roots of a sickly maple tree are creeping under the west fence, lifting up the grave of Benjamin and his son Whitefield. Their double stone is leaning forward, like a limb ready to collapse on the ground. Nothing looks the same. Everything feels the same. On a sunny April morning in 1992, the stone stood erect. An American flag fluttered in the breeze, placed there by the Sons of the American Revolution. The engraved names and dates were easy to decipher. Now the letters are smooth, nearly lost to the fungus-covered stone. The marker is dying. No flag ripples in the wind. Part of me wishes I had not returned. The Marsh cemetery needs more love than anyone seems able to give. Who will care about this place in the next generation? Will the stone eventually rest on Benjamin's bones?

As with many old Vermont cemeteries, no one takes responsibility for its care and maintenance. Although Mr. Gilman mows the grass and the Ann Story Chapter of the Daughters of the American Revolution conducts spring cleanup, the town allocates no funds to maintain the stones. Gravestones are most at risk in small family burial plots on farms in rural areas.[18]

Stretching my body on the damp grass, I focus on the fading name Foster, my maiden name. I am drawn into this stone like light into a black hole. Will I see his bones? The earth feels warm as moisture soaks my Levis.

"Benjamin, do you know me? Am I crazy communicating with you like this?" I ask, whispering so the robins don't hear me. "Why do I search for your oldest son, Ichabod? Where is his grave? Am I looking for pieces of my brother and my father?" My mind is swimming in a dark whirlpool of confusing connections.

We are a simple family. No headlines or history books speak of Foster exploits. We are one family with many branches, some broken like the maple that leans over Benjamin's marker. He was a bricklayer, a subsistence farmer who, as a grandfather, followed his young married children to the unnamed lands along Otter Creek in 1770. Ichabod followed the same pattern forty years later when he left Vermont to join his oldest son in the remote lands of western New York. Why? Is the answer entrenched in our ancestral spirits, spiraling within our DNA, embedded in the bones buried beneath me?

Crumbled leaves cuddle the stone like an old quilt, nourishing it with warmth, waiting to decay and join the bones below. What destruction have the bulging maple roots caused? Nature is pushing the bodies out of the way. I read the stone aloud as if I am telling Benjamin below me what is written above about him. My eyes lock on the last line. Died January 6, 1803. Benjamin Foster's death day, January 6, is the day of my birth. My breath catches in my throat. Why hadn't I noticed this connection before?

I push away the wet leaves with my fingers and stroke the stone. I feel as if I am crawling into Benjamin's life, watching him when he fires his musket at the Hessians. He was, for a brief period, a militia farmer, the backbone of the war in the far north. I vow to find someone who will return the American flag, plant yellow daisies, scrub the stone and stand it tall. A grave is a witness to life, an acknowledgment of existence, an honor the living bestow on the dead.

Until the mid-nineteenth century in both Europe and its former American colonies, cemeteries were merely the places to "remember, human, that you are dust, and into dust you will again return."[19]

Burial options were few for pioneers like the Fosters. People were buried in churchyards, in public town or community graveyards, or in family burial lots on their own land or land of a neighbor such as Daniel Marsh. What did Benjamin's children do with his body on January 6, 1803? The ground was frozen. His death notice appeared in the *Middlebury Mercury* on January 28, 1803.

At Clarendon, Mr. Benjamin Foster, aged 89 years.[20]

Graves confirm the life and death of my kin, their markers encasing meaning, connecting our lines, linking ones with ashes resting in a heated mausoleum in Iowa to those buried in the soil of New England centuries earlier. I study Benjamin's marker and remember that the stone for his oldest son, the center of my generational line, is missing. No records have revealed its location. Where is Ichabod?

January 1, 1813 Ichabod Foster died in the 74th year of age

Someone wrote those words on the last page of his diary. No one mentioned a burial site. He died in the unsettled lands in the Holland Purchase territory of western New York when guns were firing over Buffalo during the War of 1812. I will start my own journey west in search of his grave this afternoon.

❦

The elderly man behind the counter is still sipping coffee when I return to the Brandon Inn to pay my bill.

"I found the fort," I say. "Well, at least the cornfield along Otter Creek where it once stood."

He looks up, his eyes flashing over the rim of his glasses.

"Here, mark it on my tourist map," he says. "I'll remember, in case anyone asks."

He gives me my room receipt and jots down directions to Whiting, the small town where Ichabod raised his family after the Revolutionary War. I have reached the northernmost point of his migration trail. Eleven years ago, Ichabod's farmhouse, granary, and small barn were the only evidence of his handwork left in Vermont after more than two hundred years. Will bark beetles have eaten his cellar beams? Has the barn roof collapsed on its sidewalls? Is Belle still stirring tomato soup under the large beams in his kitchen?

I pull off the road, slip down the bank, and dangle my fingers in the cool water of Otter Creek. It bends through the valley along Route 73 toward Whiting. The noon sun dances across this gentle creek. Its flow connects, contains, and continues to nourish the history of my ancestors. I picture Ichabod on a dapple mare following this same route from Clarendon to Whiting in 1784. His oldest son guides the oxen team hauling a wagon full of cooking pots, a table, chairs, bed frames, and other household goods. Baby Ichabod curls up in his mother's lap among the bed quilts. Six other children are walking.

Settlers began returning to their land claims after the war ended. Husbands and wives who had been separated for years reunited, riding into half-familiar, half-strange clearings filled with burdocks and nettles and poplar saplings and sumacs and burnt remains of cabins. New ones were built, weeds were cut down, crops were planted, and the men and boys went back to the seemingly endless task of chopping down trees and opening up the land.[21]

I turn north at the junction with Route 30, wondering if Whiting has changed in eleven years. Soon I see a new, freshly painted sign that reads "Entering Whiting." The town is silent, like a pond without a ripple. Guy's filling station is boarded up, his grinders and gas sign gone. So is the last Whiting gas pump. The white clapboard community church is still the largest building, doubling as the home of the pastor, who doubles as the school bus driver. Across the street the post office and Bulwagga bookstore share space in a colonial house built by Ichabod's nephew, Solomon Foster, in the mid-1800s. I visit the bookstore.

A tall man with a short gray beard, wearing a brown flannel shirt and khaki pants, greets me.

"Good morning. My name is John. Can I help you find something?"

"This was a general store years ago," I say. "Where did it go?"

"It went out of business," John says. "This makes perfect space for my used books. I have hundreds to still unpack."

John had moved from New Hampshire the year before.

"Why here? Why Whiting?"

"I wanted what Whiting offers," he says. "Bucolic views, peace and quiet, and a connection with the past."

Am I searching for the same qualities?

I hand John four dollars for a book on Old English script. It will help me decipher Ichabod's diary, and remind me of a book dealer who has the courage to live simply.

The town clerk's building hasn't changed. Has Grace? The sign on the door reads "Back at 2." I park in front and wait. Soon her car pulls up next to mine. She peers through the side window. Her smile tells me she remembers. Her face is round as ever. Her hair has a few more gray strands. She climbs out, fumbling for the office keys in her purse, talking all the while.

"I have a list of the children who attended the district school in 1800," she says. "Remember Ichabod offered the land for the new school. He was paid two dollars and sixteen cents in 1808. The list is loaded with Foster children. Several were Ichabod's; others were his grandchildren and nieces and nephews."

I marvel at her memory and her energy. We sit behind her desk. Her eyes twinkle as I hand her copied pages from the diary, ones written when Ichabod lived in Whiting. Grace shoves papers aside to make room.

"Let's read aloud," she says.

We take turns. Ichabod was brief.

April 8, 1785
First robin I hear

April 10, 1785
First Marsh Quail

April 24, 1785
Frogs peep

August 29, 1790
I made my wife a pair of shoes

I had e-mailed Grace the month before to tell her I was returning and would have pages for her Whiting family history files. I was afraid to ask about the farmhouse.

October 2, 1790
First church meeting I attended in Orwell

April 25, 1791
I began to fence each of the barns

April 17, 1793
The first newspaper

August 8, 1793
Finished getting wheat into the barn

It was so cold as to freeze leathers
in the afternoon on the 10th day of April in house 1795

"I can't wait to show these to my husband," Grace says. "He grew up in Ichabod's house and his sisters were born there."

"Grace . . . is the farmhouse still there on the old Crown Point Road?"

"Oh, yes! And Belle still lives there. She is eighty-one. George died several years ago."

Those same sensations I experienced when I touched his parchment indenture return. Is Ichabod's spirit in the air, nudging me? I feel his eyes focusing on each line, his words pulling me beyond time and space.

Grace starts reading again.

a remarkabel hot day so that bees came out
of their hives and flew around as lively as
in the summer time and the snow went off so
as to leave the clear land bair.
January 22 1802

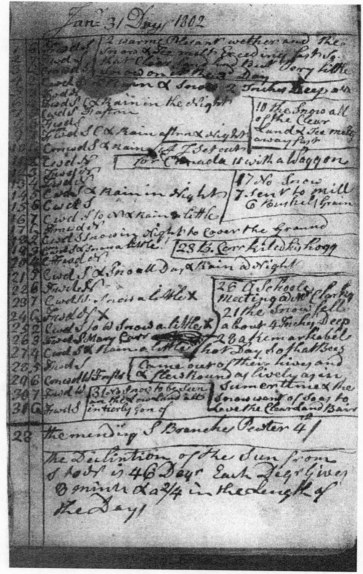

Ichabod's diary describes the weather January 1802

She tucks the diary pages into a file and labels it Foster. Then she hands me the property description. Ichabod had owned more than two hundred acres in the late 1700s. Today Belle owns only thirty-seven.

"The land is worth more than the house," Grace says. "A pipe runs from the toilet to the back field. No septic system was ever installed."

I look at Grace. Silence seals my thoughts. Our ancestors lived side by side when Ichabod was recording his daily experiences in his diary. Land deeds documenting each successive owner during two hundred years preserve our connection. Her family never left Whiting. Mine moved west. Grace's new Foster file is safe inside her vault. Ichabod's words have returned to his roots.

"I'll phone Belle," she says. "Let's see if this is a good time for you to visit."

I'm eager to read Ichabod's words to her, and to peek again at the wide beams and floorboards, to sit where he sat, quill pen in hand, writing in his diary after his children had crawled up the loft ladder to bed.

"Don't forget to come back," Grace says, waving as I climb in my car. "Give Belle a hug for me. I'll call you if the farm ever comes up for sale."

My fingers lock around the steering wheel. I look at Grace.

"What will I do if you call?" I ask, leaning out the window.

She only smiles and walks back inside her office. I know she heard me.

Chapter Three

AN EIGHTEENTH-CENTURY FARM

Silence surrounds his farmhouse. Nothing appears to have moved since my last visit. The aluminum siding still hides the boards that Ichabod attached in 1793. The barn, beaten by two centuries of penetrating wind and snow, has not collapsed. Planks, resembling crutches, still support the sagging granary.

Ichabod's granary still stands

Sumac, maple, and oak bordering his upper field form a kaleidoscope of fall colors. A crisp breeze brushes my hair. Deep within the vapors of my spirit, I imagine my hands digging into this soil, cradling kernels of corn. Was I here centuries ago? Am I wishing or remembering? The crevasse of emptiness frozen by the death of my brother and father starts to thaw. I can't explain why. Moments in time swim together, like water swirling in an eddy, circling me, releasing me. I don't remember how long I stood there.

When I first came to Vermont, I was searching for threads of inheritance that connected me to my past, seeking the earth of my ancestors. Today, that connection has a life beyond land deeds and vital records. A personality flows through the words of Ichabod. Since reading his diary, studying his sketches, analyzing his scripture notations, I have yearned to hear his voice.

Among those who have seen and felt beyond their five senses, Helen Hinchliff has said, "I really believe that our ancestors want to be found. . . . Feeling about one's ancestors, as well as thinking about them, usually results in a more successful search."[1]

I kick a couple of pebbles with my boots as once again I walk down the road toward Ichabod's farmhouse. This is the same road carved out of the wilderness in 1759 by Jeffery Amherst, commanding general of British forces in North America during the final battles of the French and Indian War. His soldiers were farmers, an "ill organized and nondescript lot, without uniforms or standard weapons. Every man brought his own squirrel rifle and such ammunition and other weapons as he could find."[2] It is hard to imagine musket fire as I walk along this empty single-track road.

My eyes drift west. Watery greens of the Champlain valley meet the purple outline of the distant Adirondack Mountains. Farmhouses like Ichabod's turned their backs on mountain views like this, facing south instead to catch as much sun as possible on long winter days.[3] Clouds creep over the far ridge. A Rutland radio forecaster had announced that gale-force winds and heavy rains would sweep across eastern New York and down this valley by nightfall.

Ichabod's upper field and farmhouse

Before I reach the porch steps, Belle opens the door. Had she been peeking through her kitchen curtains while I was photographing her farm?

"Come in," she says.

Her voice has the quiver of early Parkinson's disease. Her smooth skin, clear hazel eyes, and short, solid frame make her appear younger than her eighty-one years. She is thinner than I remember.

"Oh, it's so good to see you again," she says. She leads me into the kitchen. "Pull up a chair. I'll put on a kettle for tea."

"Belle, it is good to see you looking so well," I say. "Thanks for letting me visit again." I pause. "I'm sorry to hear about George."

"I can't talk about that," she says, turning toward the sink. The water is running.

During my first visit George had done all the talking, telling me about the outside kitchen and the original wallboards covered by plaster. He had shown me upstairs where, behind a closet door, the original steep stairs had led from the parlor to the children's sleeping space. George and Belle had unpacked their pots and pans in 1944 and never moved again.

The kettle starts to hum. Belle fusses with the teapot.

"Would you like sugar?" she asks.

"No, thank you, just plain, please."

She hands me a teacup and sits down. Faded linoleum covers the kitchen floor. Several cotton throw rugs rest on the wide boards in the adjoining living room. I try to imagine Ichabod walking across these boards toward his desk, opening his diary, picking up his quill pen. He sits erect in his hard wooden chair, sketching birds in flight, drawing books of the Bible across a page, or recording the arrival of friends. The straight, tiny rows of script often are no more than one-sixteenth of an inch high.

Baskets hang from large rough-edged support beams Ichabod had hewn by hand. They are held together by wooden pins he had carved. I pull out enlarged diary pages from my backpack and place them on the table. The originals, curling and peeling on the edges, laced together with a thin twine binding, rest securely in my safe deposit box on Lopez Island.

"I brought you pages copied from his diary," I say. "These first ones tell about the construction of fences, a garden, and a chimney before he started this house."

I hand Belle my magnifying glass.

13 July 1787
Ade a tree fence

20 December 1787
Began a chimney

1 April 1788
Made a fence and garden

20 March 1790
I set out for Whiting with my family

22 March 1790
We got safe to Whiting. I hear the first robin. Snow and wind
from the SE, wind from the N. Blessed be God we got home.

Ichabod traveled thirty miles from his log home in Clarendon to clear an acre for planting and cut timbers for a log shelter before moving his large family north to Whiting. (Abby Hemenway, H. P. Smith, and Harold and Elizabeth Webster claim that the family arrived in Whiting in 1784.)

11 April 1791
I began the log fence

25 April 1791
I began to fence each of the barns

"Two years later, he started this frame house. He completed it in 1796," I say.

Belle leans over the pages, trying to focus on the fine script.

7 November 1793
I began to hew timbers

16 September 1795
We began a stone wall east of the south of our house

December 28, 1796
We move into the new house

His labor seemed endless.

April 6, 1797
we Cleared the new Road croast our Lot on the hill East of our house

27 June 1797
We rased our Barn

5 January 1798
I Put in a glas window in the East Roome

4 December 1798
Finish the shop chimney

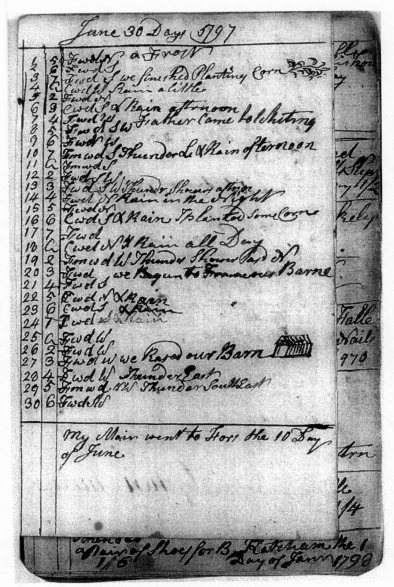

Ichabod's barn raising June 1797

"This is all so interesting," Belle says. "Where did he say the well was? Did he write about a root cellar?"

"He wrote about a well, but I'm not sure about a root cellar."

1 September 1798
We began to dig a well and finish stoning it up

"My children will love to read these words about their house," she says. "Several of them were born here. They loved growing up here." Belle pauses. She stares at the floor. "None of them stayed . . . but they call me every night."

October 1800
Susanna was born the 8 day

I was startled the first time I read this line in the diary. Ichabod recorded births, but he never mentioned names of the babies, only their fathers. Whenever his sons Benjamin or Albro or Samuel or William fathered children, he gave their first names and the sex of their children.

2 February 1810
Albro had a son born

25 March 1810
Sam'll had a son born

No parent's name appears next to the October 1800 birth entry for Susanna. Details are missing. Could Ichabod and his wife, whom he never mentioned by name, have been the parents? She turned fifty-five that year. He always referred to her as "my wife." Was Marcy, an apparently unmarried daughter, the mother? One fact is clear. Susanna lived in Ichabod's house. Vermont census records for 1800 (Whiting) and 1810 (Middletown) include her in his family. He made her first pair of shoes when she was six, and her last pair a few days before he died.

19 December 1812
I finished Susanna's shoes

Grace, the Whiting town clerk, could find no birth records for Susanna or Albro, my great-great-grandfather, born in 1785, though both appear in the diary.

16 October 1785
One of the clock this morning we have a son born

Albro was fifteen years old when Susanna was born. Parents were required to pay a birth registration fee, according to Grace. Ichabod's six other children were registered in 1783 in Vermont, perhaps before the fee was initiated.

"Do you think Ichabod's wife had a birthing room?" I ask.

"Probably so. Back there in my pantry," Belle says, pointing to a narrow doorway behind her heating unit. A square, enclosed gas heater keeps Belle warm in winter where once the hearth and central chimney stood.

We talk about this birth dilemma. We want to believe Ichabod's wife had beaten the odds, having a baby in her mid-fifties. She had given birth every two years between 1769 and 1785. Pregnancy apparently presented no problems to her or her babies.

I walk through the small door leading to Belle's pantry, the old birthing or borning room, where she stores cleaning supplies and canned goods. The beams and wide floorboards match the others in the house. The old central hearth chimney would have kept a mother and her baby warm. Deliveries were often social events in the neighborhood. Midwives were called. Other women gathered to help and to hover over mothers while they kept the men like Ichabod at a distance. Midwives were treated with dignity because they provided care to women in communities such as Whiting. Women appear in the book of Genesis as the first midwives found in literature. Beginning in simplicity, midwifery has survived through the centuries, fulfilling its meaning of "with woman" at birth.[4]

Martha Ballard, a midwife living in Maine at the time Albro and Susanna were born, kept a diary with dates identical to Ichabod's (1785–1812).[5] Her birthing accounts paint a vivid picture, as documented by author Laurel Thatcher Ulrich.

"There is a tender regard one woman bears to another, and a natural sympathy in those that have gone thro' Pangs of Childbearing which doubtless, occasion a compassion for those that labour under these circumstances, which no man can be a judge of." [6]

Martha wrote about three distinct stages of delivery: "Grinding or preparing pains, forcing pains, and grumbling pains."[7]

"Between 1785 and 1797, Martha delivered 106 women of their first babies. Of these, 38 percent were conceived out of wedlock . . . . average interval between marriage and delivery was five and one-half months . . . . Premarital pregnancy was common throughout New England." [8]

Ichabod never recorded marriages for his two girls, Marcy and Abigail, or his son Ichabod Jr. Perhaps they never married. He noted his other sons' marriages. The Ballard diary states that unmarried women would name the father at the time of birth. There is no evidence that a father was identified in Ichabod's farmhouse on October 8, 1800.

Whoever gave birth in this house that day, I picture women crowded into this birthing room behind Ichabod's hearth.

"Traditionally, the attending women at a delivery joined in a celebration afterward ('The Ladies who assisted took supper after all our matters were completed') sometimes staying the night if there was room in the house or the weather was bad. . . . There would be a clutter of beds in the kitchen and the chambers as the women fitted into the niches of an already crowded household." [9]

The Foster house was no exception. How many women had slept on Belle's floor? Ichabod wrote about rain and thunderstorms around the time of Susanna's birth. I picture her mother's Baptist friends knocking on the door carrying presents. Whether or not little Susanna was christened (Ichabod never said), her first gift of value would have been a christening blanket of fine cloth, either quilted or embroidered. [10]

I walk back into the kitchen where Belle is waiting.

"I wish Ichabod had said more," she says.

"I do, too."

He used paper sparingly, one 4½-by-6-inch page per month. Sequentially he listed the days of the month down the left side, and numbered the days of each week in a parallel column, except that Sunday, the Sabbath, was marked with an "a", not a number.

Ichabod gave a daily account of the weather without explaining the letters.

C squally snow
C snow at night

CwdS
FwdN XX
C x Rain wind NW Rain all Day

Earthquakes, eclipses, and violent storms warranted more space.

29 November 1786
Afternoon a small quake shook the earth

12 October 1792
The greatest drought ever known in these parts
since it has been inhabited and the woods very much
on fire in many places in Orwell and the towns adjacent

7 May 1805
I see a light in the air N west of the barne that
I could not account for it looked like a peace
of Barke on fire it was in the evening about nine o'clock

2 April 1807
The snow feel about a knee deepe & was a
very remarkable snow storme for the month
of Apriel as I ever knew in my remembrance
in the course of my life.

Ichabod had used iron gall ink, made from tannin (most often extracted from galls or plant matter), vitriol (iron sulfate) gum, and water. The ingredients were inexpensive and readily available. Good iron gall ink was also stable in light.[11] His paper was made from cotton or linen rags, commonly referred to as "rag paper." It had very little, if any, acid content, and is in better condition today than recent newspapers exposed to light on a kitchen table.[12]

Family and friends from as far away as Rhode Island sat around Ichabod's central hearth. I picture venison roasts simmering in an iron cooking pot, and the chimney swirling with smoke the way Ichabod sketched it in his diary. Guests pushed through the front door during a snowstorm. Others arrived in the heat of summer after a violent thunderstorm, or on a Sunday afternoon as wild flowers burst into color along their meandering stream known as Lemon Fair. Some stayed two weeks. Where had they all slept in this little house?

Ichabod recorded the travels of "my wife." During the first two years of the diary that has survived (I have no record prior to March 1785), Ichabod hardly left home. Susannah traveled without him.

9 July 1786
My wife went to Clarendon with Lucy [her sister-in-law]

22 July 1786
My wife came from Clarendon

Was she helping a sister-in-law during the birth of a baby or was she homesick for her brothers, Samuel, Hezekiah, William, Benjamin, and Daniel, who had moved from Rhode Island to nearby towns in Vermont? Ichabod recorded numerous visits.

7 July 1785
Hezekiah Carr came

22 August 1785
William Carr came to our house

20 February 1786
Daniel & Benjamin Carr

3 September 1787
My wife went to Samuel Carrs

I am stopping for only an hour with Belle before beginning my journey along Ichabod's final migration trail, leaving Whiting on the same day 192 years later. My destination is his log cabin on Lot 51 in old Willink, New York, a journey of nearly six hundred miles.

Will I be able to slip into his world, feel his seasons, his apprehension, and his emotions as I attempt to retrace his route? His diary, my guide, is void of feelings. When his younger brother Whitefield and his brother-in-law Gideon Walker died, he recorded the events in the sparsest terms, if at all.

1 November 1792
Brother Walker Died

15 September 1803
Whitefield Foster Died and Buried the 16

Ichabod never mentioned the death of his father, the Clarendon militiaman who answered the call to protect the settlers of Pittsford in 1777. All he wrote was "*6 January 1803 cloudy, wind sw   it rained in the morning,*" but the *Middlebury Mercury* noted it on the front page: "Benjamin Foster, age 87 in Clarendon, January 6, 1803." Actually, Benjamin was eighty-nine.[13]

He frequently mentioned his father's travels from Clarendon to Whiting, thirty miles one way by wagon trail, but not his burial.

13 March 1786
Father came to our house

Benjamin's last recorded visit was on February 25, 1798, when he was eighty-four years old.

Belle tucks her diary pages under her arm and walks to the counter near her electric stove. She slips them under a cookbook. As she turns, tears are sliding down my cheeks.

"I brought Ichabod home," I say. "Thanks for making room for him."

Belle smiles.

"You know, those hidden stairs you wrote about in that article[14] do not exist," she says firmly as she refills my cup. "I don't know where you got that idea. I'm sure my husband didn't tell you."

My thoughts collide like popcorn in a pot. Where did I get the idea of the hidden stairs? I can still hear her husband describing them. I know I peered down those narrow steps. I picture them as clearly as the leaves edging the upper field. Centuries ago, eight children raced through this living area and up the loft stairs to bed. (Albro's oldest brother, James Otis, died on December 22, 1776, in Rutland before this house was built.) Could my spirit have resided in one of them, or theirs in me? "It's essential to have an emotional relationship with our ancestors . . . immerse ourselves in their communities and time frames . . . they will reveal themselves to us," wrote Henry Z Jones Jr.[15] Was one emerging in me?

I climb the stairs to the loft leading to three small bedrooms where Belle's children once slept, where her great-granddaughter sleeps when she visits from Boston. Quilts, needlepoint pillows, and teddy bears cover the beds.

"You won't find a hidden stairway," she reminds me, looking up from the hallway below. "We did find a hiding place in the loft behind the south wall. That wall has been sealed for as long as I can remember."

I want to pry the nails from the plasterboard. Are the stairs behind? Grace had told me the eaves over the concealed stairs were tightly shut. She said they were used by the underground railroad to hide slaves during the mid-1800s, as other houses were in Brandon and Sudbury. Grace should know, I thought. Her husband had grown up in this house before the Senecals purchased it.

"Here, come down now." Belle says. "We can sit in the living room and visit some more."

Her living room and kitchen run together. Two small bedrooms with a bathroom in back replace Ichabod's parlor and sleeping room.

Belle sinks into her brown plaid couch. A pillow slides against her shoulder. Blue stitches spell out the word "LOVED" across the middle.

"I'm sure I can find the old photo of this house with outdoor plumbing and the summer kitchen," she says. "Now my pipes run across that back field a few feet under ground. We had to plaster over Ichabod's walls when we installed insulation," Belle says. "This coffee table was made from one of his wide wallboards."

She pauses, looks down at the table, and snuggles deeper into the couch, straightening her beige slacks and pink flowered blouse.

"Please read from your diary pages."

She reminds me of a child waiting for a fairy tale to begin.

12 October 1786
Election day

2 August 1798
voted for Representation in Congress in Whiting
M Lyon 59, D. Chip 2

10 February 1799
Mr. Lyon set out for Congress

September 1809
The Republicans had 37 vots the majority
for representative Gov't and councel this year

Vermont became the fourteenth state in 1791, the year its first federal census was taken, the one that proved by circumstantial evidence that my great-great-grandfather Albro was Ichabod's son. Ichabod made no mention of a census taker's knocking on his door, but he wrote that he voted in the federal election seven years later.

Divergent political sentiments in Vermont are illustrated by the election of 1800, when Thomas Jefferson carried every county west of the Green Mountains for the cause of the Democratic Republicans, while John Adams won the support of all those in the east for Federalism.

Ichabod first mentions Thanksgiving in 1790.

25 November 1790
Thanksgiving

However, the first Thanksgiving was celebrated in 1777, when General Washington and his army, as instructed by the Continental Congress, stopped in bitter weather in the open fields on their way to Valley Forge to mark the occasion. The Continental Congress had declared the first national American Thanksgiving following the victory at Saratoga, the day that Ichabod's father entered the militia. Washington's first proclamation after his inauguration as the nation's first president declared November 26, 1789, a national day of "thanksgiving and prayer." He simply asked for "a national day in worship and prayer giving thanks to Almighty God for the blessings bestowed upon us."[16] Thanksgiving, not Christmas, was the important seasonal holiday.

6 December 1798
was Thanksgiving

6 December 1810
was Thanksgiving in Vermont

Christmas was unimportant in the United States until the 1880s.[17] December 25 was a regular workday, which explains why there was no mention of this holiday in Ichabod's diary. He described wind directions and snow levels and little else on that day.

"What did Ichabod say about farming?" Belle asks. "I lease that lower pasture to neighbors with cows now. We used to plant corn, but no one plants crops here anymore. I only have thirty-seven acres left."

"Belle, when the Fosters lived here, your property was an active farm with over two hundred acres," I say. "Of course, not all of that was cleared. I read that most men could clear only three acres a year. Here are some farming entries recorded when he was building this house."

27 April 1792
I set apel trees

20 July 1792
Sheered our lambs

8 August 1793
Finished getting wheat into barn

14 August 1793
Burndt my fallow

30 May 1795
I began to plant corn

During Ichabod's time, farmers could raise twenty to thirty bushels of wheat per acre and forty to fifty bushels of corn, with some crops yielding as much as seventy to eighty bushels an acre. Farmers in Clarendon, where his brother Whitefield lived, raised two hundred to five hundred tons of excellent hay per season.[18]

I imagine Ichabod would have carried grain and fruit seeds from Rhode Island. He would have harvested sour, astringent-tasting wild apples that were very rarely edible by today's standard. Although the seedling fruit from the orchards was small, crabbed, and tart, it was used for livestock feed and for producing cider and vinegar. A few settlers brought with them grafting skills known and practiced from Roman times. Ichabod was one of those who practiced the procedure.

2 May 1795
We graft apel trees and set them in a nursery
west of the house on the Spaulding lot

With top or cleft grafting, cuttings from a neighbor's most desirable fruit-bearing seedlings were placed on the branches of a grown tree. This process produced individual branches, which would continue to produce the preferred fruit year after year. In bud grafting, a bud from a tree bearing the desired fruit was placed at the base of a one- or two-year-old seedling tree. This bud grew out, eventually replacing the original branch, creating an entire tree of the desired variety.[19]

With these methods, Ichabod and his neighbors could upgrade the produce of their own seedling orchards. He continued to apply his grafting skills when he reached western New York, adding grapes to his list when he was seventy-two years old.

Ichabod built his own lime kiln.

May 1795
I labored on the lime kill 2 days

7 June 1795
We set the lime kill a fire

Burning limestone, which is calcium carbonate, produces quick lime (calcium oxide). By adding this to his soil, Ichabod would raise the pH, thus improving its fertility. Quick lime was also used for building mortar.

Clearing land in Whiting was difficult. In the southwest part, where Ichabod lived, the land was valuable but covered mostly with hardwood trees—maple, oak, ash, birch, and elm. Hardwoods had little value at the time except for fuel or construction. Excess wood, including stumps, was cut and hauled by oxen onto great piles, then burned. Ashes from hardwood trees were saved to make lye, which could either be used to make soap or boiled down to produce potash.[20]

His family would wash their hands, faces, and feet with lye soap weekly and probably take one bath a year. Outer clothing was seldom washed, just the underclothing once a week.[21]

Belle and I sit quietly. She looks out at her bird feeder in the front yard. I lean back in my chair and close my eyes. Images move softly through my mind of the upper field full with corn, a patch of melons creeping across the grass, tomatoes hanging on vines near the front window.

After a few moments, I ask, "Now that Guy's store is closed, where do you buy your groceries?"

"Oh, people bring them to me. My children help."

The nearest grocery store is fifteen miles east in Brandon, the mill town where Ichabod took his corn to grind into mush for making samp. I smile.

Ichabod never faced Belle's dilemma. His family grew their own carrots and peas, cucumbers and potatoes, corn and cauliflower; raised pigs and cows; baked their bread; and churned their cream into butter. The Fosters' three daily meals were undoubtedly very much alike: pea and bean porridge, salt pork, and samp (cornmeal with milk or water).[22]

Ichabod's wife would have cooked stew in her Dutch oven that would swing on a bar and hang over the fire. She probably had a spider pot, too, with legs to keep it off the coals. The boys would butcher their hogs when winter came, smoke them, and store them in a barrel outside. Ichabod was a self-sustaining, organic pioneer by necessity, not by desire for an alternative life style.

I start reading again.

10 June 1785
The spotted cow took the bull

22 July 1790
Red cow went to bull

6 November 1791
Killed a hog

17 November 1793
We killed our hogs

At butchering time, Ichabod and his boys would have removed the bristles, filled a big iron kettle with water, and built a fire of pine knots and stumps. Most of his pigs would have been kept until they were very fat, so there would be plenty of salt pork. The hams and bacon were smoked over a slow fire of corncobs in his smoke house.[23]

24 April 1798
We framed and rasied a smoke house

Livestock, in the absence of fences, ran wild in the woods. Cattle were branded or earmarked to indicate their owners. Ichabod had registered his mark with the Whiting town clerk.

12 August 1794
Our earmark a half crop the under
side of the right ear

He made shoes for his family and relatives, including boots for the men and slippers for the women.

29 August 1790
I made my wife a pair of shoes

13 June 1793
I made John boots

20 June 1793
I made Marcy shoes

1795
It was so cold as to freeze leathers in the
afternoon on the 10th day of April in our house

The shoemaking trade was brought from England. Thomas Beard, a London shoemaker, arrived in Salem, Massachusetts, in 1629, several years before Ichabod's great-great-grandfather, John Foster, settled there in the old north fields along the Ipswich River. Freezing winter snows and mud, rain, swamps, underbrush, and hard stony ground of the New England wilderness would quickly wear the strongest shoes and boots beyond repair. Cobblers were the ones who mended shoes. They traveled and were highly trained and well paid.[24]

Most colonists either couldn't afford the high prices or didn't want to wait the weeks or months for their orders to be filled. Many learned what they could from the shoemakers and made their own shoes. If the shoemaker was a farmer, he simply punched holes through the rim of the uppers and the sole, slammed tiny wooden maple pegs into them with one hammer stroke each, and greased them with tallow if they were work shoes.[25]

Ichabod could make a pair in one day. He would have sat near his hearth with a smooth flat lap stone and pounded the leather of the sole with a metal hammer and a wooden mallet. Sometimes he might have added a clog to help keep his sons' feet out of the mud. The sole would have been made of tough, thick cowhide. The heel might have had hobnails to keep the shoes from wearing out too quickly. The "uppers" would have been two pieces of coarse leather somewhat softer than the sole.

4 November 1795
I made Ichabod & Albro shoes

6 September 1797
I made shoes for B. Ketcham

15 July 1799
I had a tub made for a liquor tub for dressing of leather

4 December 1806
I made mySelf a Pair of Shoes

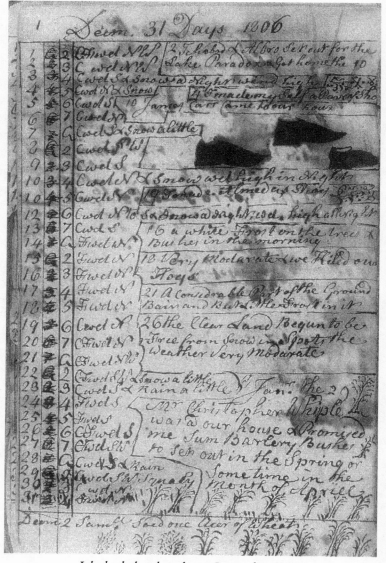

Ichabod sketches shoes   December 1806

The first time he mentions making shoes for his two young-est boys, Ichabod and Albro, they were ten and twelve years old. Did they go barefoot until then? Often boys wore dresses until they were old enough to work in the field. Then they changed to long pants and, apparently, put on shoes.

While Ichabod made shoes and planted corn, his wife and daughters, Marcy, Abigail, and perhaps Susanna, would have picked wool and carded rolls, spun yarn and driven looms to make cloth. They would have cut, sewn, and mended all the garments for their family of ten; dipped candles and made soap; milked the cows and fed the calves; and "gone visiting and to meetings on their own feet," [26] carrying their only pair of shoes in their hands to save wear until they approached the meetinghouse.

"This diary of your Ichabod is amazing," Belle says. "He was an educated man."

"Yes, I think he was. He educated his children, too. Grace showed me records indicating that both Ichabod and Benjamin had children enrolled in Whiting schools in the early 1800s."

Before the period of district schools, a woman often opened her home to young children like John and Benjamin Foster to teach them reading and arithmetic when they weren't needed in the fields. These were known as "Dame Schools." Little money changed hands in those days; the teacher probably re-ceived her pay in vegetables, eggs, and pork. Ichabod's boys might have cut her firewood.

By the early 1800s, the Vermont legislature voted to have all towns divided into school districts. Whiting had three. Ich-abod donated land for his district's school.[27]

28 February 1803
The school was begun in the house south of Clarks.

At the close of the Revolution, the only paper money available was almost worthless. The result was a universal resort to barter. In 1786, the Vermont legislature recognized wheat, rye, and Indian corn and other items as legal tender. Wheat especially was used in meeting notes, contracts, salaries, even taxes.

"Belle, without currency from cash crops, neighbors along your road exchanged goods and services they needed to survive," I say.

15 July 1785
I gave Docker Reed a note for two bushels
of Indian corn to be paid
the first day of December next.

11 April 1791
I took 15 sheep of Elijah Right to pasture and
he is to pay my town rate
to Pliny Smith

14 August 1793
Borrowed Indian meal from Mrs. Spaulding 7 1/2#

"Doctor Reed and Elijah Right were frequent visitors to this farm," I say.

12 May 1795
I sold our spring wheat

"This entry tells us he succeeded in growing more than his family needed, and apparently received money for it," I say. "Maybe that is how he purchased leather to make shoes."

"My children will be excited about all this," she says. "I've searched for my Fogler relatives, the ones on my mother's side, but I haven't gone back as far as you. Finding our ancestors is so comforting."

"Would you mind if I look in the root cellar?" I ask.

"Why would you ever want to do that? I never go down there. George always checked things for me."

"I think it is the only part of the house I haven't seen."

"Well, I'll wait for you."

The cellar door creaks, as if it doesn't want to let me through. A small shelf above the top step contains cans of peas, beans, peaches, assorted pickles, and a flashlight. A musty odor burns my nostrils. I cough. I switch on the flashlight and creep down the stairs. Dusty cobwebs dangle from the wooden beams. Ichabod had left their bark alone. I reach up and run my fingers along a crusty edge. Did I touch his thumbprints? Beetles have burrowed inside the wood. Moisture hangs from rusty water pipes and sagging electrical wires. Cloudy pools dot the dirt floor. I slip on a plank as it slides into the mud. I seem to be creeping into a Charles Addams cartoon.

I stop and circle my light around the cellar. I spot a stone foundation lined with brick. Iron support rods shore up the ceiling in places where Ichabod's beams have fallen. This cellar, like the rest of the house, is a hybrid of renovations, witness to generations of change, supported by his original design. I notice stones framing a wooden door at the far end. My great-great-great-grandmother would have entered there, carrying an apron full of apples, her hands calloused, a fall sun slipping across the back of her muslin dress. Suddenly, this dismal root cellar reveals a maternal purpose.

"Are you all right?" Belle asks. "Please be careful."

She must have walked to the top of the stairs in the kitchen.

"I'm fine. I'm coming up now." I whisper a prayer that a short circuit doesn't ignite these dry beetle-infested beams some winter night. Belle takes my hand on the landing and leads me back to the living room.

"Here, let me wipe those cobwebs out of your hair."

She sinks into the couch again. Her eyes droop. A west wind rattles her bay window, which had replaced Ichabod's front door years ago. Dark clouds roll across the sky. I should leave and let Belle rest. This graceful great-grandmother loves Ichabod's house as I do and embraces its endurance and strength. She and I are linked to the life of a common man whose work and words are stitched into our own lives. She has allowed me to look behind her doors and around her corners, inhaling my family history. I long to crawl up those loft steps and curl up in a quilt. I say nothing.

We walk to the side porch in silence. Belle wraps her arm around me. We hug. I walk to my car door and turn back to say good-bye again. Two robins land on her bird feeder. I squeeze my hands together and whisper, "Yes! What was, still is!" The robins still return to the Foster farm. Unchanged. Ever changed.

19 March 1786
First Robin I heard

For twenty-two years, Ichabod kept track of the robins' arrivals in the spring, along with frogs peeping, carrier pigeons landing, Canada geese flying over.

Belle looks through the lace curtains as I drive slowly down the old Crown Point Road. The farm fades in the distance through my rear window, its sagging granary and leaky barn, aged to soft grayish red, disappear. I don't want to move on.

A voice inside me whispers, "Claim his house and his last thirty-seven acres for your family." Should I save this Foster farm, like an heirloom purchased to pass on, before history plows it under? Will someone ever etch the name Foster on Belle's mailbox? Should I return to my roots, surrounded by the peace of this place, and plant corn, listen for the first robin, and keep a diary of daily events?

Aluminum siding has replaced his clapboards, a bay window covers the original front door, wide boards are hidden behind plaster walls and rolls of linoleum. Ichabod would not recognize his house. What had he left behind, hidden by contemporary coverings?

16 October 1811
Rain a little Ichabod came into Whiting with a waggon

17 October 1811
I set out from Whiting with my family and effects for the
Holland Purchase in York state

Slowly my foot pushes down on the accelerator. I notice Lemon Fair, the creek marking his western property line, a few hundred yards ahead. A lump chokes my throat. How did Ichabod feel when he closed his front door for the last time, leaving cultivated fields behind to start over in the untamed forests in the Holland Purchase lands of Willink in western New York? His hands had carved the pins that held his kitchen beams in place, pounded the iron nails for the siding. His lateral saw had fashioned the floorboards.

Did tears trickle down Susannah's cheeks when she looked over her shoulder at her hearth where she had prepared samp for breakfast, baked bread in her beehive oven, perhaps birthed a baby named for her in the warm room behind? Twenty-two children had called her "grandma" by the time she climbed into the wagon with her husband and their effects.

What effects would fit? Ichabod didn't leave behind his shoemaking tools. He cobbled shoes and boots until two weeks before he died. They must have packed clothes, and pots and pans. Did Susannah take her spinning wheel and carder, necessities for turning flax into cloth? What was she forced to leave behind besides her friends, children, grandchildren, brothers? Ichabod packed writing paper, pens, and a supply of ink.

His diary migrated with him. Without it, I would never have known who he was, what he valued, how he lived, or where he died.

I imagine Ichabod, his white hair and long beard limp in the damp air, helping Susannah crawl into the wagon. She pulls a wool shawl over her shoulders and cuddles an eleven-year-old in her lap.

When I decided to follow their route from Whiting to Willink, I wanted the season to be similar to theirs. They picked the end of October. So did I. However, I am traveling in a car protected from the harsh weather they encountered. I will reach Willink in five days. It took them five weeks.

I had highlighted their route on my Vermont and New York road maps. Ichabod named Middletown and Poultney, Argile and Broadalbin, Brutus and Geneva, Clarence and Buffalo. In fact, he listed twenty-six communities where they stopped for the night or "lay over" if snow was falling or rain made the trail impassable. Some towns don't appear on current maps. He mentioned the families who gave them shelter and hot meals during their journey. Ichabod walked. So did twenty-eight-year-old Ichabod Jr. Susannah and eleven-year-old Susanna rode in the wagon. They traveled twelve to fifteen miles a day, if the weather permitted.

Why did they attempt this long, arduous journey over ruts, rocks, and few roads, across streams without bridges, through drizzle, rain, and snow, as winter approached? The first snow had already touched the corn stalks in Whiting. Ichabod was seventy-one, Susannah, sixty-six. My age. They had been married forty-three years. So have I. Ichabod was my husband's age. Those same sensations of serendipity slip under my skin.

Chapter Four

ICHABOD AND HIS FAITH

I stop on the narrow bridge that crosses Lemon Fair. Ichabod's farmhouse is a white dot in the distance, framed in fall foliage. Few people travel the old Crown Point Road anymore. I haven't seen another car since I turned off Route 30. I stand on the plank bridge and watch the calm water. Weeds choke the stream where Ichabod was immersed with his Baptist brethren.

23 September 1790
Seventeen Baptised in the creek

He was fifty years old. I picture him standing in this creek, his gray beard dripping, his blue eyes looking to the sky, his ears listening for the peeping frogs he recorded each year in his diary. His church's Meeting House stood a few hundred yards up the hill in the neighboring township of Orwell. He may have joined this church to avoid paying the required taxes of his father's Congregational church or because there wasn't yet a Baptist congregation in Whiting.

2 October 1790
First church meeting I attended in Orwell

Along with Susannah and their eight children, he would've walked across this bridge each Sabbath. They were barefoot, carrying the shoes he'd made. Their footwear had to be clean, no mud or manure sticking to the soles, when they entered the Meeting House. He became a devout member, even hosting religious events in his home.

29 May 1793
A day of fasting and prayer at my house

He never planted corn or harvested wheat on Sunday, the day marked each week by an "a" in his diary. Settlers couldn't leave their houses except to go to and from the public worship of God on the Sabbath. No one cooked after sundown on Saturday.[1]   Church law forbade driving a team on the Lord's Day, which explains why the Foster family would've traveled to church on foot. Their travels were easier after Ichabod built this bridge.

1 July 1798
I made the bridge to Orwell

During my first visit to Vermont, I discovered his church's minutes stored in the vault of the Orwell Town Hall. The formation statement was dated December 24, 1787, long before Christmas Eve was a Christian celebration. The founding brethren wrote:

> . . . *considering ourselves a feeble band, and in remote circum-*
> *stances. . . . taking into consideration the importance of the lovers*
> *of the Truth as appearing as lights in the world; a motion was*

made whether it might not be for the honor of God, and for the mutual peace and comfort of our own souls that we should form ourselves into a visible church state, and for this purpose proposed to open our minds to each other.[2]

Ichabod wasn't one of the eleven who voted to organize in 1787. Two years later, his name appears on the membership rolls along with eleven members of his family. However, the year he completed the bridge must have been a hard one for him. In the minutes for December 6, 1798, the word "excluded" appears after his name and that of his son John Foster. Elders held power over both religious and civil decisions resulting from complaints brought to their attention by members. Elders "deliberated officially concerning the individual derelictions of [their] flock." [3]

Brother Ebenezer Willson complained against brother Reuben Smith for marrying a second woman before obtaining a bill from the first. Sister Owen complained about Alice Cartrite for backbiting, slandering and falsehood, which, being supported, we proceeded to withdraw the hand of fellowship from said Alice.[4]

At this time a number of brethren manifested dissatisfaction with Brother Rathbun and Sister Sabra Chamberlin, and from this time our troubles began to creap on.[5]

Churches governed the lives of these early Vermont pioneers. The church and state were one. Complaints continued against members for lying and using unseemly language. The elders dismissed many members. Some withdrew on their own, joining Ichabod and others who had "previously erased their travel with the church." How could the "mutual peace and comfort of their own souls" outlined in their founding mission statement disintegrate so quickly?

The church minutes describe incidents regarding Brother Gregory and Brother Flagg and their failures to honor contracts with the Fosters. Ichabod recorded one response in his diary.

December 1797
I went to Elder Warren's and he appointed Wentday the 3 Day of January 1798 to attend to Bisness that concerns us.

However, he never recorded the matter in his diary on January 3 or any other day. Instead, he turned again to reading his Bible from Genesis to Revelation.

1 April 1798
I finished reading the Bible through in course BIBLE

19 August 1798
*This day I finish reading the old testament
in course the second time*

20 October 1798
I finished reading the Bible in course the second time

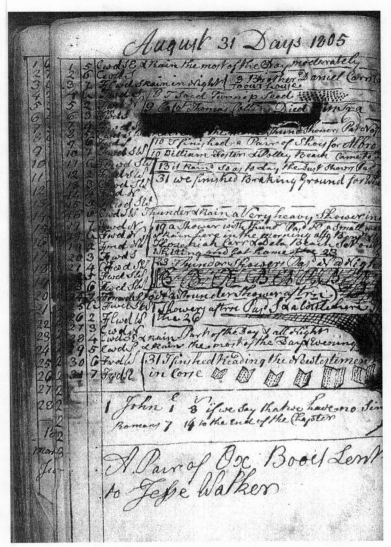

Ichabod sketches books of the Bible   August 1805

I sit on his bridge, remove my shoes, and touch my toes in Lemon Fair. I close my eyes and imagine the day Ichabod determined he could no longer "walk" with his brethren. I see him stomping out of the Baptist Meeting House, his eyes blazing, his small frame sinking into the deep Vermont snow, the wintry wind chilling his cheeks. Susannah remains behind with their children. Swirling snow buffets him as he turns east and starts down this narrow track road leading to their farmhouse. He slams the door. He slides his chair closer to the hearth and picks up his Bible. Did he find comfort in one of his favorite verses recorded years earlier in his diary?

17 September 1790
The lord to me a Shepard is want therefore shall not. I be in the
paths of Rightous for his namesake lead me

For the creature was made subject to vanity, not willingly, but by
reason of him who had subjected the same in hope

What had gone wrong with the Baptists? Did Ichabod feel shunned when Elder Webster excluded him? Had he walked out first? When Susannah and their children arrived home after Sunday services that day, were angry words spoken or kisses shared in the parlor? Ichabod didn't express emotion in his diary.

His son Benjamin, a married man with a young family, brought his personal problem before the elders on November 31, 1799. The Baptist minutes read, "Brother Benjamin Foster exhibited a complaint to the Church against Brother Ebnr. Flagg for receding, or falling from a contract concerning a piece of land."

He entered a similar complaint against Brother Gregory and, like his father, walked out of the church over the decision of the elders. They said Benjamin's complaint was ground-less. Ichabod and his son John renewed the complaint against Brother Gregory to no avail.

The next year, Elder Webster had second thoughts about excluding Ichabod and John. He and five others in the church hierarchy visited them on August 6, 1800.

Attended to hear the report of the committee chosen to visit brethren Ichabod Foster and John Foster. Report of the committee was that they found them complaining against brother Gregory for rendering a corrupt judgment in a certain arbitration; but again it was the unanimous opinion of the Committee that their complaint was groundless.[6]

The disagreement surrounding Brother Gregory remained an unresolved issue for Ichabod.[7]   During his years of exclusion from the church, Susannah traveled with the elders to meetings. Did that cause a rift in their relationship? Was she in Hartford for nearly two weeks?

19 February 1796
My wife set out with Elder Brown for Hartford in York State

5 March 1796
I sent for my wife to Hartford

Susannah never resigned her membership or behaved in a manner to warrant exclusion by the elders. I imagine she walked barefoot to Sunday meeting with her daughters in tow, leaving Ichabod at home to read his Bible alone, never allowing the men and their financial disagreements to dis-suade her from "attending to the mutual comfort of our souls."

The Fosters weren't the only brethren at odds with the elders. Brother William Fisher claimed Brother Peabody Thayer exhibited the following immoral and un-Christian characteristics:

> *Imprudent loose carriage, giving occasion to suspect unchastity.*
> *Unkind treatment towards his wife.*
> *Refusing to hear or attend to the second step of labor using hard words disclosing an ugly disposition.*[8]

Elders were slow to decide issues. The Fosters' first complaint took five years to resolve. Ichabod never budged, never reversed his decision to leave the church. His great-great-grandparents, John Foster and Martha Tompkins, had escaped persecution by the elders of the Anglican Church of England, and settled in Salem, Massachusetts, around 1635. Charles I, king of England, granted them freedom to make their own laws.[9]

These Puritans wanted to purify the Church of England of what they considered extravagant frills, such as colorful robes, prayer books, and stained glass windows—the gaudy, gilded decorum of the church—and replace them with prayers from the heart and sermons crafted by the local preachers from deep and prayerful study of Scripture.

Ichabod's ancestors believed women and men were equally capable of joining the church, receiving grace, and entering the kingdom of heaven. These early Puritans had a very low tolerance for domestic discord and high expectations of peace and harmony, traits exhibited during Ichabod's membership in the Orwell Baptist Church. I'm sure he smiled the day his friend and neighbor Deacon Murray accused the powerful Elder Webster of falsehood.

30 September 1804
The Council set in Orwell on Elder Webster's account and he was
found guilty in the matter brought forward.

Elder Webster was excluded on October 5, 1804. According to the Baptist minutes, the council found him guilty of improper behavior during a meeting in Woodstock, Vermont. Church elders spent years recording civil complaints, seldom mentioning spiritual issues.

Ichabod didn't walk into a Baptist Sunday meeting again until after he moved south to Middletown in 1805. Tomorrow I hope to bow my head in prayer in that same church.

Drops of rain brush my cheeks. I pull my toes out of the water and dry them on the jacket I'm carrying. My Levis are damp from drizzle I hadn't noticed falling. I feel anchored to this place where Ichabod felt the baptism waters drain from his face, where he listened to the peeping frogs. I hear a sparrow chirp. Could these splintered boards I'm touching be ones Ichabod pounded into place in 1798? That same psychic connection returns. Is his spirit watching me?

I slip behind the steering wheel. The weather is changing. Broad streaks of creamy white light stretch across the sky, banking against coal-black clouds arching behind the Adirondack Mountains. I stop at the spot where the Orwell Baptist Church once stood. I've driven my first mile west. Nearly six hundred lay ahead before I reach the hamlet of Concord in the village of Willink. The lot is vacant, the congregation deceased, living only in the words of its minutes. Accounts of misdemeanors, baptisms, and complaints involving the Foster family between 1789 and 1805 are secure in the vault at the Orwell Town Hall.

I continue through town and turn south on Route 22A. Where will I sleep tonight? Middletown has no motels. I wish

I had asked Belle if I could sleep in the loft. Will she slip the diary pages from under her cookbook—ones that tell about the building of the barn and the smokehouse, the quilts Susannah sewed, the corn kernels planted in her fields, the baby born in her pantry—and read them to her children when they call tonight?

Cold drizzle pelts my windshield. I switch on the heater. Ichabod recorded rain, too, and snow. I imagine him slipping in the mud and slush, hanging on to the side of the wagon. The Fosters must have shivered in the cold. In the early 1800s, few New England wagons had covers.

21 February 1805
I set out with part of my family and affects for Middletown
and got their the same day at night safe through the
Divine Goodness of God.

27 February 1805
Benjamin came into Middletown with his family and Sam and
wife and child, also Amos Walker with wife and mother and
Lucy Beach came with Benjamin

Turning east at the junction with Route 4, I detour to Rutland. I might find a motel there. I notice the Town Hall. I slip two quarters into the parking meter and run up the steps. Rain rolls down my back. I sign the register. A tiny, middle-aged woman wearing a brown flowered dress and dark-rimmed glasses leads me to the vault, a narrow, windowless room crowded with men dressed in business suits conducting title searches.

"You can't look at vital records," she says. "The woman in charge is out sick. However, you can look at land deeds. We close in thirty minutes."

"Thank you," I say. "The Foster Revolutionary War pension records and birth registrations indicate they stayed around Rutland during the war. I hope your grantee-grantor land index will validate my assumption."

She points to a tall card catalog.

"You won't need the same land deed volumes as these men," she says. "You'll be looking through the ones listing the earliest land purchases and sales before Vermont became the fourteenth state."

Cards in the file list Fosters and the dates of their land activity. Each one tells me the volume and page where the deed appears. I find eight transactions involving Ichabod between 1772 and 1793, including four during the Revolutionary War period. Others name his brothers Joel, Benjamin, and Whitefield. The earliest one for Whitefield is dated September 10, 1768.

"Now I'm convinced Ichabod didn't take his family to safety in western Massachusetts, but probably stayed inside the Rutland fort during Tory raids," I say.

"You may be right." The woman stays at my side, pulling out the volumes and setting them on the table.

"I don't get many requests for these books," she says. "I enjoy meeting people with history. Someday I'll take time to search for my family."

"Can I copy Ichabod's deeds?"

"Yes, but let me do it," she says. "These pages are fragile. I'll hurry. My office closes shortly."

I feel rushed and tired, but grateful to find a woman who will take time to help me.

"Come back on Monday and you can look through the vital records," she says, handing me the deed copies.

"I wish I could, but I'll be traveling across New York State by then," I say. "I'll contact you if I need additional documentation. You've been very helpful."

She smiles. "Good luck with your search."

I walk down the steps and cross the street to my car. The rain has stopped. My stomach is growling for something more than granola bars and water on the run. Flashing lights advertise a Chinese buffet and a movie theater in the Rutland plaza across the street. I forget about finding a motel. The movie complex features *Under the Tuscan Sun*. I have enough time for a quick Chinese dinner before the next showing. I treat myself to a steaming plate of fried rice with beef and snow peas. My mind plays back images of the Pittsford battlefield, the graves in Marsh Cemetery, the root cellar in Ichabod's house. Green tea relaxes my nerves. I've had a full day.

I slip into a center seat in the theater. Few people are attending this early-evening showing. The strain of taking notes, reading Old English script, and talking melts away as the green hills and rows of olive trees fill the screen. The story of a woman's adventure, her courage to start over, to tackle a new challenge in a foreign land, releases the tension I feel in my shoulders. I slip back in my seat, alone but not lonely. Was this protagonist on the screen a modern-day Susannah?

As the credits roll, I remember I don't have a place to sleep. I rush to my car and find my map. The main route through Rutland must have some motels. Headlights streak across my damp windshield, reflecting light off the wet blacktop as I turn right onto Strongs Avenue. It's dark. Suddenly, ether-like images surround me. Ichabod and Susannah, their sisters and brothers, their children, their in-laws, people whose names I'd read on land deeds and gravestones—Gideon Walker, Thomas Collins, Hezekiah and Benjamin Carr—appear in ghostly haze. I stop on the side of the road, afraid to drive on.

No one touches me. Their faces are strong, narrow, with long noses and sharp chins set adrift. Why are they covered in flowing black capes? Are they saying good-bye or hello? Does it matter? I feel them thanking me for honoring them for who they were—are—recognizing their hardships in the wilderness, their courage and sorrow.

I'm scared. The images hang there for several moments. Are they traveling silently in my subconscious? Are they haunting me? They make no demands. Jack-o'-lanterns and goblins light up nearby store windows and front porches. Halloween is approaching. The residue of a long day is piling up in the graveyard of my mind. Since breakfast I have tramped across battlegrounds, searched for graves, found new Whiting records, shared the diary with Belle and Grace, and rushed through Rutland land deeds. My eyes burn, my shoulders hurt. I pull back into traffic and turn south on Route 7. The images slip away; the memory remains. Why does this visual sensation feel real? Have I uncovered a sixth sense not governed by time, space, or appearance? Have I found fluid ground without boundaries, a new place with baffling dimensions? Will I ever see Ichabod again?

I can't share this phenomenon with my children. They'll roll their eyes and (secretly, so as not to hurt my feelings) decide I need watching.

I find a room at the Red Lion Inn on Route 7 and fall asleep in minutes after slipping into my pajamas. The sun wakes me the next morning before 8 o'clock. It's Sunday, the day marked "a" in Ichabod's diary. I return to my detour point and pick up Ichabod's trail to Middletown. A narrow mountain road follows Poultney Creek to Middletown Springs. "Springs" was officially added to the name in 1885 after fresh water sprang forth following a massive flood that raced down this creek in

1868. An earlier flood in 1811 may have contributed to Ichabod's decision to move west.

Middletown Springs is like many whitewashed Vermont towns that grew up around 1790 and hardly grew again. Its largest population was 1,068, recorded the year before the first flood. Ichabod had moved, following his disagreement with the Orwell Baptist Church, with his faith apparently intact. The community has one all-purpose store where residents buy milk and butter and day-old newspapers. The trees on the surrounding mountains are bare. Dead leaves from the oak and maple, birch and ash await the first snow for burial.

I park in the lot next to the white colonial-style church and climb the steps, smiling at parishioners whose eyes tell me they wonder where I came from. They nod, say nothing. I remember Grace telling me strangers aren't hard to spot in these parts. Middletown boasted two churches when the first flood washed away the town's businesses. Today there is one. Is this Ichabod's Baptist church?

I slip into a pew near the back, hoping no one else will notice me. My knees bend toward my chest, reminding me that people were shorter two centuries ago when this church was built. I feel a tap on my shoulder. A bubbly, round-faced woman leans over the pew. "What is your name?" she whispers.

She tells me hers and introduces her husband, a trim Englishman wearing a white tennis sweater of the 1950s with a red geometric patterned tie tucked inside. His sideburns and handshake convey a sense of importance.

A young man strums an electric guitar and leads a four-piece combo through contemporary versions of traditional hymns. Children scamper up and down the aisles. A baby squirms in her mother's lap in front of me. About fifty people are worshiping in a space that could hold three hundred. Suddenly, the walls reverberate with "Holy, Holy, Holy! Lord God Almighty." I sing as loud as I can, as if I want all my ancestors who worshiped in Middletown to hear me. If I sing and pray and read Scripture where Ichabod did, will I feel my roots reaching deeper into our shared connection? I hope the power of the old pipe organ conceals my exuberance.

I doubt that Ichabod heard organ music in the Baptist Meeting House 192 years ago. I don't know if his small congregation could even afford the services of their minister, the Reverend Sylvanus Haynes, who married my great-great-grandparents, Albro Foster and Rispa Doane.

15 June 1806
Albro was married in the after part of the day

When it comes time to lead prayers and offer a few inspiring words, the sporty Englishman sitting behind me steps forward. He's their reverend. After his sermon is over, he looks at me and asks, "Would you mind telling us who you are and why you are here?"

People turn. I want to sink into my pew, but my knees won't bend any more. I can't hide from his question. I lick my lips as I fumble with words to frame a reply; nothing is simple for Ichabod or me.

"I'm from Lopez Island, Washington," I say. "My great-great-great-grandfather attended the Baptist meeting services here in the early 1800s before he moved west."

I'm an oddity in this small back-mountain town, a woman traveling alone. Not many people come through this tiny community at the base of Haystack Mountain laced with grade-four gravel roads leading to communities even smaller. Soon the story I have repeated often on my journey flows with ease, like a stream in spring.

"His family lived up the mountain road behind this church, the one leading to Ira," I say. "Ichabod helped build the Middletown Baptist Meeting House. His diary says he carved pins for the structure."

I mention neighbors named in the diary, wondering if any descendants live here now.

"He left Middletown with his wife and two of his children 192 years ago," I say.

Oohs and aahs erupt from women wearing simple hats. Eyes hang on every word. Will Ichabod be the centerpiece of next Sunday's sermon?

"I'll leave this afternoon to trace their route west to Willink in western New York."

A baby starts to cry. I thank them for listening and sit down. The reverend leads us in a closing prayer and the benediction.

Young couples and elderly women shake my hand as we file out.

"I am a Carr. I wonder if we are related?" asks one young mother.

"Be careful," says a white-haired woman wearing a wool coat.

"You know, there is a Foster Road right up where your property was," says a teenage boy.

A man wearing a flannel shirt, Levis, and boots stands back until everyone else has passed. He doesn't seem to have family in church.

"You want to see that old Baptist Meeting House of your ancestors?" he asks. "It's right across the street." His brown eyes twinkle, as if he has a secret to share.

Does he mean this white church was not the one Ichabod attended? I feel sad as I slip past the few people standing by the front door and follow his quick steps across the commons.

I don't remember seeing another building resembling a church when I arrived.

He turns to me as we cross the road. "That's it," he says, pointing to a blue-shingled, two-story structure. No door. No steeple. The building looks neglected. I don't know what I feel. Shock? Disappointment?

"The Baptist Society sold it to a potato farmer in the 1930s," he says. "He stored potatoes inside for years until I bought it."

We walk around back. The wind tosses leaves around stacks of old barn boards. Crows cackle in the branches overhead. Slivers of white ice are forming along the edges of a puddle beside the building.

"I restore barns," he says. "Come, I'll show you inside."

The barn-like door won't slide. He runs back to the church to find the man who last had the key. I follow.

"Can I change into my Levis and boots in the church restroom while you search for the key?" I ask.

"Sure. I'll show you where it is and meet you back here."

He is digging in the dirt beside the door when I return.

"I'm looking for the key," he says. "It is supposed to be under this bucket."

I kneel on the ground and dig under the leaves. My hair and skin feel oily. The inn had no hot water this morning. I smile, remembering that Ichabod and Susannah probably bathed only once a year. I keep digging. Dirt cakes under my nails.

"What's your name?" I ask.

"Dan McKeen. Did you know this building was built in 1816?"

"No, it wasn't," I reply. "Ichabod's diary said it was raised in 1806. I can show you. I have a copy of that diary page."

We stop looking for the key and walk across the road to my car, retracing our steps between the living church and the deceased one. Dan reads the diary lines:

26 & 27 June 1806
The Baptist Meeting House in Middletown was rased

"I can reappraise the building," he says. "It's worth more than I thought. Can I make a copy of this page?"

I hand it to him. He goes inside the church before the reverend locks the doors. Moments later, Dan returns with four copies of the diary page and the door key. I don't ask where he found it.

He rolls the large sliding door. The noon sun slips through cracks in the wallboards. I try to imagine Ichabod singing inside this building on the day he left for Willink. A rusty potato conveyer belt runs up one side. Tall boards line the opposite wall. I can't picture the famous Reverend Sylvanus Haynes preaching to his Baptist flock under this roof, or Ichabod praying in this space, or the elders pronouncing judgments here.

"It used to have a second floor," Dan says, "but the potato farmer took it out."

"What were pins?" I ask, picking dirt from under my nails. "Ichabod wrote that he made pins for the Meeting House."

25 June 1806
I made Pins for the Meetinghouse

"Pins held this building in place," Dan says. "This is what Ichabod would have made." He hands me a piece of wood about eight inches long, rounded and tapered to a point. Next he picks up an ax and splits a small piece of wood in four sections. He sits on a bench, reaches for a two-handled sharp-edged saw, and locks one piece into a wooden vise.

"Watch me. This is how Ichabod would have made his pins."

A minute later, Dan hands me two new ones.

"Take these on your trip," he says. "Might remind you of Ichabod's time in Middletown."

Dan invites me to sit on the bench with him.

"You have time to talk a bit before you move on?" he asks. "I mean, about old times in Middletown? Seems we each want to bring it back, or at least see that it is remembered."

"Do you recall hearing about the horrible flood the year Ichabod moved west?" I ask.

"Everyone knows about that. That's the day that killed this town."

The morning of that flood, Ichabod and Susannah would have awakened to a day similar to this one, bright and clear. Their house was northeast of the town square, bordering on a small stream in the hills near the Ira town line. Eyewitness accounts of the flood reported that about nine o'clock a black cloud was seen rapidly rising in the west, accompanied with thunder. The rain soon fell in torrents, and so continued to fall until the latter part of the day. It seemed like a succession of thunder showers following each other without intermission and what may perhaps be considered as remarkable, the heavy rain was confined to the town of Middletown and the west part of Tinmouth.[10]

I can't picture the panic that must have gripped Ichabod and Susannah when the Poultney River and mountain streams near their house suddenly overflowed with raging rainwater. Thunder booming. Lightning flashing.

"The little stream which rises among the hills in the north part of town [where Ichabod lived] was ordinarily so small that fording it even is unnecessary to cross it—a mere step in many places is sufficient—had suddenly swollen to the dimensions of a large river, stretching to 75 feet across in parts." [11]

"Four gristmills and three sawmills, three distilleries, two or three clothiers, several mechanics' shops, two taverns, two stores, and several homes washed away. With the buildings went several hundred bushels of grain, a quantity of lumber and much other property. The stream rose so suddenly that little was saved. Hogs, numbering 100 or more [on a farm below Ichabod's house], went down the stream and were scattered along from Middletown to Poultney, wherever they happened to be driven ashore. Some came out alive, but most of them were drowned. Great injury was done to the land on those streams. Some portions of the meadow lands were cut up and washed away." [12]

"Let me read you what Ichabod wrote about the flood," I say, pulling a diary page from my folder.

22 July 1811

There fell such abundance of water that it swelled the greater criek with the streams in Middletown, Poltney, Ira and Carelton as to destroy mills, forges, carding machine factory, dwelling houses, tan works and all the grain and grass on the intervails on the streams and three lives was lost.

Ichabod's house survived. Others didn't. Sixteen stranded neighbors slid across a thin rope to safety before their house broke apart and washed downstream. A good many men were thrown out of employment. The livelihood of much of the town was carried downstream.[13]

"I photocopied Ichabod's land deeds during my first visit to Middletown Springs in 1992," I say. "I found his property near the Ira line. His house was gone by then. I believe he returned to his farm in Whiting shortly after that."

I tell Dan I had driven up the hill along the old road, following the little stream that had become a seventy-five-foot-wide river, carrying pigs to their death three months before Ichabod moved west. I had trudged through overgrown brambles and prickly weeds and peeled back a piece of bark from the large birch tree growing inside the remains of Ichabod's stone foundation. Unlike his Whiting farm, no buildings remain.

"I had tucked the bark in my shirt pocket," I say. "I don't remember why. Whenever I find my ancestors' land, I feel compelled to collect something, a handful of black dirt, a twig, a small stone, something free and in some form that may have been there when they farmed the land."

"I feel that way when I buy an old barn to restore," Dan says. "I am touching the past. Someone's past, anyway. If you acquire his Whiting farm one day and want to restore his barn, I'd like to work with you."

"I hope that can happen," I say.

"Your Ichabod would have used these, too, when he built his Whiting house," he says, handing me six hand-pounded iron nails. "The heads on these old ones have a roll-like design. The flat heads were made later."

"Thank you, Dan. He mentioned nails in his diary."

October 1797
Borrow of Jen Halle 1 3/4 lb of single nails.

1 November 1797
Lent him clapboard nails

Dan slips his business card into my pocket. I watch him pick up the diary page telling about the Meeting House, the one that assures him this old Baptist church was worth more than he thought. He pins it to a wall lined with newspaper clippings, sketches, pinup girls, jokes, and assorted cards and memorabilia. Is Ichabod smiling at his diary page nestled next to a photo of Marilyn Monroe, his script flowing across her bare legs? Are his church elders frowning?

"I'll carry the pins and nails back to Lopez Island," I say. "Thanks, Dan, for taking time to show me your building."

Frost has formed on the edges of my windshield. I shiver as I imagine what Ichabod's family felt as they climbed into their wagon, hugging their friends in front of the church. Ichabod turned his oxen west as snowflakes slid down his nose.

I return to Route 140, following the creek back to Poultney, where Ichabod spent his first night after leaving Middletown.

24 October 1811
We set out with our family and effects for the Holland Purchase.
Stayed in Poultney that night. Snow

I pull into a gas station. While the tank is filling, I study my map, locating the route through Hartford, Argile, Saratoga, and Saratoga Springs. I had downloaded an 1810 map. Matching it with a current map of New York State, I'm amazed how many of his small towns exist today. Back roads connect them. The New York State Thruway bypasses them.

25 October 1811
Went to Hartford

26 October 1811
Went to Argile Force

27 October 1811
We drove to Saratoga

I'm on my way to the Genesee country. My next four days are unscheduled. As I approach the New York-Vermont state line, a sign on a barn reads "Take Back Vermont." Will I return someday to take back the Foster farm?

Chapter Five

WEST TO WILLINK

I wind along Vermont Route 31, connecting with Route 149, crossing the border, picking up New York 22A at Granville. Could this be the route Susannah traveled with Elder Brown the time she stayed nearly two weeks, the time Ichabod sent for her to come home?

I arrive in Hartford in twenty-five minutes. Ichabod walked the nineteen miles from Poultney in one day on his way to Willink.

25 October 1811
Went to Hartford

The township, founded in 1793, feels deserted, as if time flew over and never looked back. Leaves creep across the road, breaking the silence. I park beside a cemetery. I'm hoping to see someone I can ask about the families buried here. No one steps out onto a front porch to say hello. Is the caretaker peeking around the lace curtains in his parlor? A box at the gate contains a directory of graves. Ichabod's diary says his wife's brothers, Samuel and Daniel Carr, settled in the area in the late 1700s. During the winters of 1797 and 1798, Ichabod's children traveled back and forth from Whiting to Hartford numerous times. He never said why.

20 February 1797
Benjn, Wm and Marcy set out with their Unkel & Aunt for
Hartford in York State

2 March 1797
Benjamin & Marcy got home from Hartford in York State

10 March 1797
Benjn set out for Hartford in York State

7 December 1797
Benjamin got home from Hartford York State

1 February 1798
Wm & Abigal Foster set out for Hartford York State

13 February 1798
Wm Abigal Foster & Abigal Carr got home
from Hartford York State

16 February 1798
Ben set out for Hartford in York State

22 February 1798
Ben & John got home from Hartford in York State

The name Anna Carr appears in the cemetery directory, but I can't find her headstone. Was she Susannah's sister-in-law, cousin, a niece, an aunt? A pot of yellow mums marks a new grave. I lean against an oak tree and bite into a granola bar as I recall the details of my search for Susannah's family. I found the Rhode Island vital records books in the Seattle Public Library one Saturday shortly after locating Ichabod's diary on the

Internet. The first page I opened under Washington County, Rhode Island, births from probate records, 1685–1860, read:

Carr, Benjamin had wife Mary and children Daniel, William, Samuel, Hezekiah, Benjamin, Susannah, Penelope, Abigail, Freelove & Deborah all under age ment his will dtd 6 July 1762 pvd Ex 14 Sept. 1762 Ex 2:173.[1]

Among the hundreds of pages in that volume, why had I turned to this one? There was no index. Benjamin's will designated items for his wife and all the children. For Susannah, his oldest girl, he wrote, "I give unto my beloved Daughter Susannah one feather bed and beding when she comes to the age of eighteen years of age." Benjamin and Susannah were common names, but I felt this Susannah was the right one. She was living in Exeter, where the will was probated, when she married Ichabod of Coventry in 1768. Her age at her death, recorded in the diary in 1820, validated this assumption. She "died in her seventy-fifth year," making her seventeen, "under age ment," when her father died. All her brothers' names, identical to those in the will, appear numerous times in the diary.

Ichabod was meticulous about recording everyone's visit to his house.

16 November 1789
Brother Samuel Carr & wife

20 May 1791
Brother William Carr

14 February 1792
Brother Daniel Carr & his wife

April 1792
Brother Hezekiah Carr

14 March 1800
Brother Benjamin Carr & his family got into Whiting from Ira

I was confident the published Carr family history books would substantiate my discovery. However, not one book mentions Benjamin and Mary and their ten children.[2] In fact, Susannah is listed in several accounts as Ichabod's widow, who allegedly married Spinks Tarbox in 1770. I was angry. Ichabod didn't die. Why would anyone print something like that? Genealogists call these dilemmas brick walls, where one is stymied, can't see a way through, but somehow keeps looking for an opening. I had copies of deeds in which Ichabod and Susannah sold land in Rhode Island and purchased land in Vermont after the date of her alleged second marriage. I kept digging. I found French and Indian War accounts, land transactions, church and marriage records that tightened my argument.

Several days earlier, when I was leaving the Manuscripts Department of the Rhode Island Historical Society library, I had stopped at the main desk to show the librarian Ichabod's Vermont indenture, which Karen had copied for me. On her counter was a book titled *Descendants of Roger Williams, Book III: The Sayles Line Through His Daughter Mary Williams*.[3]

I don't know why I picked it up. I have no connection to Roger Williams. I don't understand why I stopped at page 11. Suddenly I was reading the genealogy of Susannah's father, Benjamin. I stared at the librarian and asked why the book happened to be there on her counter. She said she didn't know, but these things happen all the time around here.

She guided me to more evidence. *The Diary of Samuel Tillinghast of Warwick, Rhode Island 1757–1766*[4] tells about Uncle

Caleb Carr and the death of Benjamin Carr, with a date matching the date on the probated will.

August 27, 1762
Cloudy Wd S'y. Had fine Showers of Rain. PM
fresh Wd S'y. Thick clouds. [second entry] Fryday
this day PM Died poor Benjaman Carr After a long and
Tedious Illness with many Disorders [36] ye 23 Instant I Took
my finall farewell of him, and Such a picture of Patience I
hardly Ever See before.

August 29, 1762
Still Continues Drizle with Some Showers. Wind Esterly [third
entry] Ye 29th D [Sunday] [Benjamin Carr] was buried in his
own land whare he dwelt.

Susannah's family goes back to the governor of Rhode Island, Caleb Carr, and to Roger Williams. Benjamin Carr was Susannah's father, the son of Caleb Carr and the brother of Caleb Carr (who named a son Caleb). It gets convoluted. Captain Tillinghast's diary made me wish Ichabod had been more forthcoming with descriptions, but he did give me a valuable clue. Ichabod wrote a letter to Benjamin Carr's brother Caleb (Susannah's uncle) just before he died in Warwick, Rhode Island.

17 October 1792
I rit a letter to Unkel Caleb Carr

A chilling breeze blows across the Hartford cemetery. I stand up and shake grass off my pants. My legs are stiff. Should I walk across the street, knock on the door, and ask if any Carrs or Fosters live in Hartford? Locating living relatives while searching for the dead ones, talking to descendants with names like Carr, Doane, Prouty, Walker, Randall, Washburn, Beach, and more enlivens my family quest. Searching for my ancestors is like having a disease for which there are no antibiotics, just stimulants that put a smile on my face. Brick walls can tumble down when one finds a preponderance of favorable evidence. I have reached that threshold of truth regarding Susannah's family.

Ichabod's only previous trip outside Vermont was to Hartford. The town was formed from what was then known as Westfield (now Fort Ann), six years before Ichabod arrived. It received its name from early settlers from Hartford, Connecticut. "The roads for these early pioneers were blind paths whose general direction was indicated by blased trees."[5]

7 March 1799
I set out for Hartford with my wife & Samll & Almedia,
12 went to Brother Daniels [Carr]
15 went to Widdow Browns & Mr. Halls,
16 stayed Mr. Vendwsee
18 we got home from Hartford in York State

The Baptist Church lists Daniel Carr as a member in Hartford. Was "Widdow Brown" the wife of "Elder Brown"? Ichabod hardly left Whiting, noting rare trips to mills such as Brandon and visits to family in Clarendon and Ira.

20 November 1786
I went to Clarendon

28 May 1790
I went to Clarendon

29 May 1790
I went to Ira

Was he frightened on his first night in New York? Did he regret leaving his settled Vermont landscape? This westward journey wasn't a one-day excursion to a neighboring town but a five-week trip over single-track plank roads and rutted trails through mostly unsettled lands foreign to him. Fortunately, his son Ichabod had completed one round trip to Willink and, like his brother Benjamin, returned safely.

13 March 1811
Ichabod got home from Welink near Lake Erie

I decide not to disturb the quiet of the Sabbath in Hartford. It's four o'clock. I need to keep driving. I have two more villages to pass through before reaching Saratoga Springs, a college town where I hope to find a room.

Ichabod stopped next at Argile Force.

26 October 1811
Went to Argile Force

I can't find it. I follow Route 40 to Argyle, a town swallowed up by expansion. New York starts to feel disorganized, like a militia without a plan of attack. I make my first of many wrong turns before finding the back road to Saratoga, the place where General Burgoyne surrendered on the day that Ichabod's father raced to protect the Pittsford settlers.

Ichabod records his route to Willink October 1811

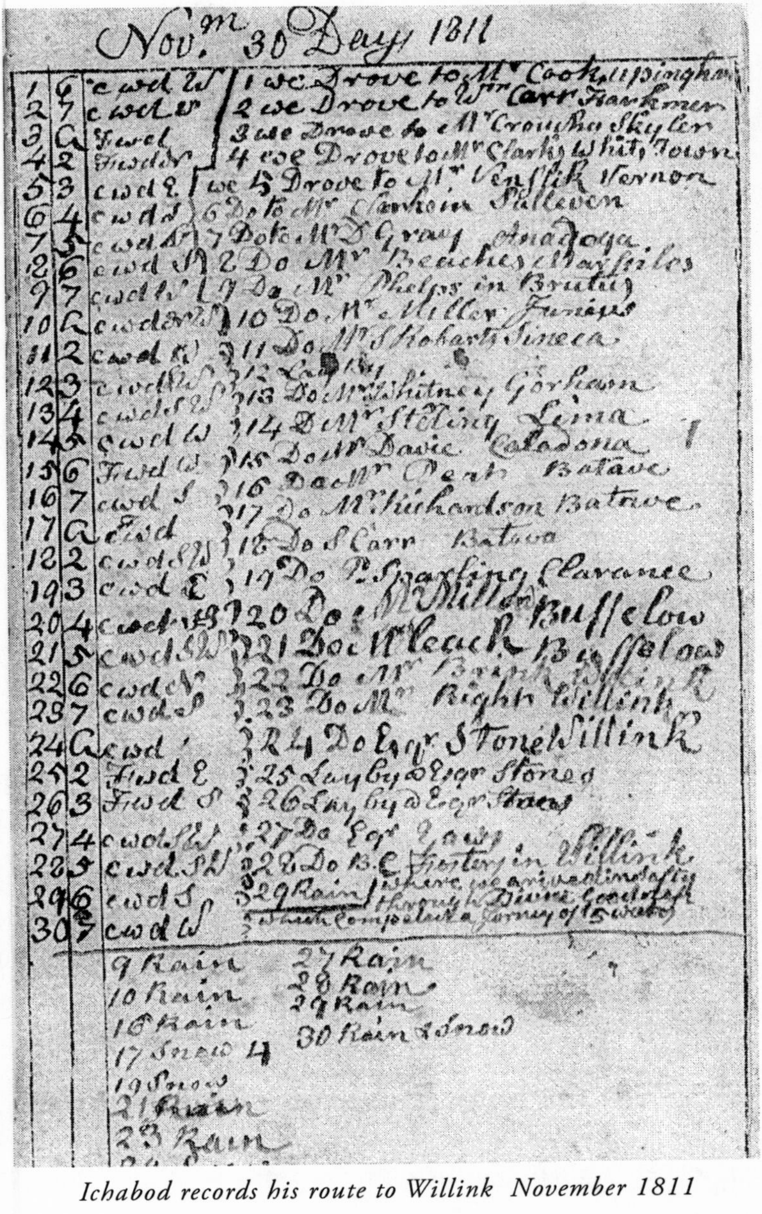
Novm. 30 Days 1811

1 6 cwd W 1 we Drove to Mr Cook Mssingham
2 7 cwd W 2 we Drove to Wm Carr Harkimer
3 G Fwd 3 we Drove to Mr Crouch's Skyler
4 2 Fwd N 4 we Drove to Mr Clarks White Town
5 3 cwd E we 5 Drove to Mr Venslik Vernon
6 4 cwd 6 Do to Mr Clarke in Sulleven
7 5 cwd S 7 Do to Mr D Gray Onadoga
8 6 cwd S 8 Do Mr Beaches Marsiles
9 7 cwd W 9 Do Mr Phelps in Brutus
10 G cwd 10 Do Mr Miller Juniws
11 2 cwd W 11 Do Mr Stoharts Sineca
12 3 cwd 12 Lay by
13 4 cwd S W 13 Do Mr Whitney Gorham
14 5 cwd W 14 Do Mr Steling Lima
15 6 Fwd W 15 Do Mr Davie Caladona 1
16 7 cwd S 16 Do Mr Pert Batave
17 G Fwd 17 Do Mr Richardson Batave
18 2 cwd S W 18 Do S Carr Batava
19 3 cwd E 19 Do P Sparling Clarance
20 4 cwd 20 Do Mr Miller Buffelow
21 5 cwd S W 21 Do Mr leach Buffelow
22 6 cwd N 22 Do Mr Brush Willink
23 7 cwd 23 Do Mr Right Willink
24 G cwd 24 Do Esqr Stone Willink
25 2 Fwd E 25 Lay by at Esqr Stones
26 3 Fwd S 26 Lay by at Esqr Stones
27 4 cwd S W 27 Do Esqr Laws
28 5 cwd S W 28 Do B.C. Fosters in Willink
29 6 cwd S 29 Rain where we arived in safty through Divine Goodness
30 7 cwd W which Compleated a Jorney of 5 weeks

9 Rain 27 Rain
10 Rain 28 Rain
16 Rain 29 Rain
17 Snow 4 30 Rain & Snow
19 Snow
21 Rain
23 Rain

Ichabod records his route to Willink November 1811

Burgoyne had suffered one thousand casualties in the fighting of the previous three weeks, while American losses were fewer than five hundred. After a miserable march in mud and rain, Burgoyne's troops took refuge in a fortified camp on the heights of Saratoga. There, an American force that had grown to nearly twenty thousand men surrounded the exhausted British army. Faced with such overwhelming numbers, Burgoyne surrendered on October 17, 1777. By the terms of the Convention of Saratoga, the members of Burgoyne's depleted army, some six thousand men, marched out of their camp and stacked their weapons along the west bank of the Hudson River.[6]

I stop on the same west bank to read the marker, one not about the surrender but about a barge operated when Ichabod and his wagon full of the family's possessions crossed the river. He spent the night here. Saratoga isn't named on my map. Today it's called Schuylerville.

27 October 1811
We drove to Saratoga

Rain pounds on my windshield, like the rat-a-tat of a hammer hitting small nails. Headlights blur my vision. My mind is a muddle. What do I expect to learn by driving across New York that I don't already know about Ichabod? I feel foolish following his route. I can't locate original towns. His landscape is gone. I can't duplicate the cold and fatigue he must have felt. Saratoga Springs is eleven miles from the original Saratoga. Soon I am driving along Broad Street past Banana Republic, the Gap, and Eddie Bauer. I stop at Starbucks, where a girl behind the counter gives me directions to a bed and breakfast on Union Street and calls ahead to make a reservation for me.

Soon I am soaking in a hot bath; my latte resting on the rim of the tub reminds me of my home near Seattle. Bubbles

trickle down my neck. I wonder how Ichabod felt on the night
he reached Saratoga Springs. Did blisters erupt on his heels?
Was Susannah's head pounding? Was her stomach upset? A
wagon ride could churn cream into butter.

I wrap a towel around me, pick up a magazine, and flop
down on the bed. Triple windows with tieback curtains line
the back wall of my second-floor room. A desk, dresser, and
lounge chair complete the furnishings. I find an article about
a woman who spent time meditating on her ancestors while
on a pilgrimage to India. Am I on a pilgrimage, too, meditating on my ancestors? I close my eyes and try to imitate the
author's practice. My shoulders sink into the pillows. Soon I
am dreaming of a family dinner. Those same sixth-sense feelings surface. This time my mother and father, my brother,
Jake, Aunt Mabel and Uncle Ellery appear. Others arrive. No
food has been served. We expand the table, making room for
Ichabod and other ancestors who slip into the room, just as
they floated into my vision on that rainy night in Rutland. I
appear as a child, sitting next to Ichabod.

Where do dreams live? Which senses define reality? Is
death a line on the horizon that we cross over seamlessly, back
and forth, through timeless time and spaceless space, like the
ever-moving cycles of the moon? I brew a cup of tea and crawl
under my covers, blessing my relatives wherever they reside.

Frosty air dries my lips and chills my fingers as I unlock my
car door the next morning. I am anxious to move on. I expect
Ichabod was, too. I find old Route 29 leading to North Galway, Broadalbin, and Johnstown. Ichabod's words are my road
map. He walked fifteen miles to North Galway, and an amazing

thirty-two miles on the following day, before he reached Johnstown at night in the rain.

29 October 1811
Drove to North Galawy

My defroster melts the ice on my windshield. Ichabod would have felt every raindrop and snowflake that hit his nose. I yearn to slip inside his skin, feel the strain of his calf muscles tightening as he endures another hill, hear his encouraging words to his tired daughter, smell his presence. I feel blessed with the peace this back road offers and the opportunity to drive alone, allowing my thoughts and questions to unfold uninterrupted. My imagination can write the script he neglected to include in his diary.

Why am I following his footsteps? Am I seeking a connection with kin, keeping family together? Was he? Are graves the glue that seals this connection for generations?

I can't find North Galway, so I drive on a few miles to Broadalbin. Ichabod didn't stop overnight, but his family had made many trips here. Benjamin, his son who settled on Lot 51, spent eleven weeks living in the area with someone in 1809. He was too sick to travel on to western New York.

28 February 1809
It was the first time I heard of Benjamin after he set out for Sandy Creek by the information we have he was so sick when he got to Newgallway that he was not able to go any further

2 March 1809
Samuel, Lydia and Hezekiah Carr set out for New Gallaway to see Benj.

7 March 1809
Samuel got home with a load of salt and brought news of Benj being some better

15 March 1809
Sam'l set out for Broadalbon

1 April 1809
*We rec'd a letter from Br. Beach in Broadalbon which
informs us that Benj. is better*

2 April 1809
Br. Beach was at our house on his way home from Broadalbon

16 April 1809
*We rec'd a letter from Dr. Rawson in Broadalbon which informs
us that Benjamin is regaining his strength remarkably & that we
. . . thankfully acknowledge of the goodness of God toward us*

19 April 1809
Ichabod [junior] got home from Broadalbon

24 April 1809
Sam'll set out for Broadalbon in Y Stat

30 April 1809
Benj got home after eleven weeks . . . in Broadalbon in Y. State

Dr. Rawson had arrived in Broadalbin from Connecticut
in 1805. He was the town's first physician and became a leading citizen.[7]

The numerous family trips to Broadalbin and Benjamin's
lengthy stay there suggest that he must have been seriously
ill. Dysentery, influenza, typhus, measles, smallpox, pneumonia, and scarlet fever were common diseases. Did Dr. Rawson
treat Benjamin with frequent bleedings that would "free" the
body of poisons and restore its balance with nature? Early doctors believed that illness was brought on by a lack of harmony
with nature. Imbalances among the four humors—blood,

phlegm, yellow biles, and black biles—led to symptoms of disease.[8]

I cross the Kennyetto Creek and stop at a small park. A granite marker under the shade of several trees reads:

These trees are planted in memory of Dr. Byron E. Chapman 1892–1965; Dr. John G. Butkus 1908–1969; Dr. Richard D. Kearns 1918–2002. They are warmly remembered as the last house call doctors in the village of Broadalbin. They always came when needed.

A lump forms in my throat. Family scenes drift through my mind again. I remember my father sliding back his chair from the dining room table, picking up his black bag, and leaving on another house call. I was six years old. My brother always sat across from me, my mother at the end. I hardly recall an evening when my father didn't visit several sick children and calm the nerves of worried parents. He, too, was one of the last doctors to make house calls. Born in 1897, he started his calls in 1922 when he finished his training in pediatrics.

I imagine Dr. John Morgan, reins in hand, making a horse-and-buggy house call to the Iowa homestead farm where my father contracted polio in 1909. The Washington County doctor gave him a quarter the day he raised his arms above his head. My brother and I were our father's guinea pigs for the Salk and Sabin vaccines when polio was finally contained in the 1950s. He vaccinated his other patients next.

Ichabod protected his family and friends from infectious diseases, too. He inoculated them against kine or cow pox.

22 February 1811
I innocalated Mr. Sherman, Albi Collins, Jarvis
Rastus with the kin pox

1 March 1811
I inoculated Angline, Avelin & Marcy with kine pox

10 March 1811
I inoculated Angeline and Sally Smith

Because of the distances between settlements and the un-
availability of medical expertise, every man was his own doctor.[9] The only thing Ichabod mentioned suffering from was
St. Anthony's Fire, named because the affected skin area became bright red. He recorded remedies for different medical
problems.

1 September 1797
To Stop Blood take Common Narrow dock [plant that grows next
to nettles] roots powder and apply to the wound

March 1799
Receipt wound that is bad and does not work well,
take comfrey root [medicinal plant] and pound till it is a poltis
and lay it on the wound It seldom fails to set a wound to work
soon. It is very healing.

October 1799
Fire weed is good for the pile . . .

December 1801
A remedy for a Cancer [corn] take Narrow
Dock roote and boile it
in water and bath the Cancaer with it and then pound into a
poltice after boiled on the sore—an Indian Medicine.

February 1803
For a cancer take oile olive and rub it in a
copper vestal new tined
and simmer it until it has a consistency of an ointmen.

August 1803
For blind piles [inside the skin] hop roots, boil down strong
then sweeten the liqor with west India molasse.

December 1804
to stop blood use Beach Barke, Canada Lice, Red Nettel
Strong Vinegar, Salt peter & Mum gun Powder

I thought Ichabod was a genius until I read these identical words in almanacks and newspapers published by Anthony Haswell of Rutland in the 1790s. He copied many verbatim. His great-grandson, Harry Hinckley, was the first officially trained doctor in the family. He graduated from medical school in Chicago in 1898, the year after my father was born. Harry's mother, Ann Jeanette Foster Hinckley (the woman who saved Ichabod's diary after her father, Albro, died in North Eaton, Ohio, in 1874), mortgaged her Kansas farm to pay her son's medical school bills.

I leave Broadalbin and continue west on Route 29. The fertile Mohawk River valley stretches before me, like a landscape painting overflowing with silvery water, crystal skies, and verdant fields. Why didn't Ichabod and his children settle here? Why did they travel hundreds of miles farther to reach Willink? I pass a yellow clapboard building beside the road.

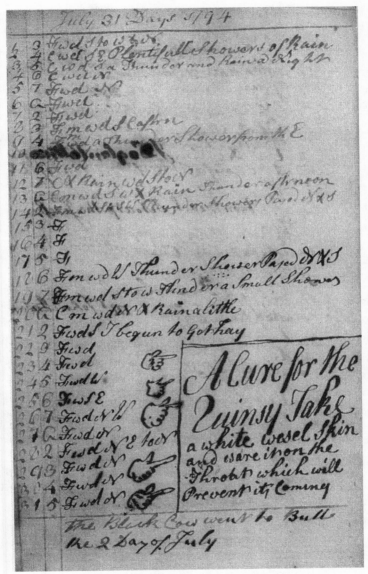

Ichabod records his medical remedies September 1797

A sign reads, "Nellie Tavern 1741." I realize Ichabod had entered a state settled long before Vermont land became available for indenture. The Indian trader John Lydius was living south of here when he met Ichabod in 1761. This valley had been claimed before the Vermont wagons began to pass through.

> . . . *one of the principal motivators for their leaving was the allure of free or cheap land. Thus, as they migrated, they tended to skip over areas that were already settled, because the choicest lands, along rivers and major routes, were claimed by the earlier arrivals. New Englanders started moving west in large numbers beginning in the 1790's, most passed right through the Hudson and Mohawk valleys, in favor of unclaimed lands further west.* [10]

I get lost in Johnstown. Ichabod must have had a better idea of where he was going than I do. I resent drivers tailgating me when I am trying to find the right road through town. I pull over to the curb and jump out before a UPS truck leaves.

"I figure with your map that you need some help," the driver says, leaning out of the window.

"Yes, and I figure a UPS driver knows all the roads."

The young man laughs.

"Where is Route 67?" I ask.

"That's simple," he says. "Go back to Main Street, right down there by the second light, take a left, and you'll run into it."

"Thanks."

"Glad to help," he says. "Where are you headed?"

"Buffalo." Willink would not appear on his route map. It has four different village names now.

"Why aren't you on the New York Thruway?"

"I'm trying to follow the original route west carved out by the Mohawk," I say. "That's the way my family went in 1811."

"Oh, you're one of those genealogy buffs," he says. "My mother is searching for her great-grandparents over the Internet."

"Is she having any luck?"

"I don't know. I'll ask her tonight. I better get back to my own route, the package delivery route," he says, rolling up his window.

Ichabod covered thirty-two miles in the rain and wind on this leg of his route. He stayed an extra night. Mr. Aveedon is the first person named in his nightly notations.

30 October 1811
We drove to Mr. Aveedon's in Johnstown & in rain in the night.

31 October 1811
Rain all day & we lay by all day

A short way past Johnstown I connect with Route 10, then head west again on Route 67, which soon becomes Route 5. It's after two o'clock. My back aches. I haven't stopped for a sandwich. The country is rolling, the road is straight, bordered by farmland when not consumed by urban sprawl. I can see the New York Thruway on the other side of the Mohawk River. I vow not to resort to the fast track. I push on.

Ichabod's next stop was Bingham. I can't find it. Maybe it doesn't exist anymore, or has another name, or I'm translating his diary wrong.

1 November 1811
We drove to Mr. Cook in Bingham

2 November 1811
We drove to Wm Carr in Herkimer

Could William Carr be related to Anna Carr of Hartford or to Ichabod's wife? Should I stop at the town hall? Because birth and death records were not kept in New York State until the late 1800s, I continue on. Ichabod's diary said nothing about the people or the countryside. His words let me imagine what it was like for him and Susannah, young Ichabod and little Susanna. I'm sure Ichabod carried a gun. Deer, bears, and wolves were plentiful. The year he signed his Vermont indenture with John Lydius, his grandfather, Samuel Day, left him his musket.

His will, dated 11 March 1761, reads:

I Samuel Day of Attleboro [Massachusetts], yeoman make my will . . . to my daughter Rachel wife of Benj. Foster a feather bed . . . to grand son Ichabod Foster my muskett.[11]

Was Ichabod's namesake carrying that musket when they started west to Willink? Samuel Day's will dismantled another "brick wall." The Day family's records claim that Rachel's father was Benjamin Day, not Samuel. The will proved otherwise.

3 November 1811
we drove to Mr. Crouches in Skyler

From Herkimer to Schuyler, Route 5 is straight and flat along the Mohawk River. Ichabod probably paid a barge fee to cross the river here. He was on the well-traveled Mohawk – Genesee trail now. In 1794, a road from Old Fort Schuyler (now Utica) through Canadaigua to the Genesee River was laid out. The route of this old Indian trail eventually formed the connection between the Hudson and Niagara Rivers and was completed in 1809, two years before Ichabod's journey.

Traffic lights blend with sunlight, blinding my eyes as these towns start to run together.

4 November 1811
we drove to Mr. Clark's in Whitestown

In Utica, I ask for directions to Whitestown. No one seems to know. There is a Whitesboro, which doesn't appear on my 1810 map. A woman in the Credit Union parking lot directs me through Utica, a city laced with fast-food restaurants, traffic lights, bridges, and four-lane roads. Vermont was so much simpler. I notice the large sign for Whitesboro. Nothing for Whitestown. I was expecting a community left behind as Whiting and Hartford were, with its name slightly altered since Ichabod had passed through. Instead, I'm locked in rush-hour traffic.

In my confusion over the town's name, I miss my turn. I am heading north on Route 5 when I need to find the right route west. I pull off into a Penske truck rental lot. A burly man with a two-day beard tells me to keep going north. I say I want to go the other way, the back way, the old Genesee road. I'm not looking for the New York Thruway. I don't want to waste time telling him why. He relents, rubbing his head, and finally tells me the old way to Vernon.

5 November 1811
Mr. Griffith   Vernon

I'm still on Route 5, staying south of Syracuse, as the sun disappears.

6 November 1811
Mr. Clark   Sullivan

7 November 1811
Mr. Gray Anadoga [Onondago]

I worry that I'll miss another road sign. Ichabod would have worried about bears attacking his family. I'm distracted by flashing lights and crushing lanes of traffic, wondering where I will be by dark. Once I'm across the Mohawk River and back on the old Genesee Trail (some places call it the Seneca Turnpike), the country is shaped by rolling hills, deep valleys, and high ridge lines. I glance to the right. The view from Diamond Hill melts away the tension in my shoulders. A giant body of water shimmers like a mirage in the fading light, miles away, across the fields. Is it Oneida Lake? I'll check my map when I stop. I find Route 13 and turn south. After several miles I turn west on Route 173 and left again at the junction of 175, which leads me into Marcellus. Ichabod had only one route to find. I have more than I can keep track of.

8 November 1811
Marcellus   Mr. Beach

Marcellus, founded in 1792, honors its beginnings with historic storefronts, hand-painted road signs, and an old cemetery near the main square. I park by the Historical Society. It is closed, open only on Thursdays. This is Monday. I walk toward the small market to ask directions to an inn. A woman tells me there is no place to stay in Marcellus, not even a bed and breakfast. New York is taking on that remote feeling of Vermont.

I find Route 20 and push on another eight miles to Skaneateles in the dark. I have no place to stay. The inn on the main road is full. I follow a sign south on Route 41A and turn into an old estate farm with a large red horse barn and manor house. My head pounds as I trudge up the front steps with my backpack slung over my shoulder. Karen, the Hobbit Hollow Farm innkeeper, says she has a room for me. I promise myself I won't push so hard tomorrow. I curl up on my bed in a room that looks like a slice of pie. I'm facing a bay window looking north with panes angling to each side—one to a lake, the other to a horse pasture.

Thunder rolls out of the west. Black clouds blow past. Wind rattles my windows as rain pours off the ledges. The weather can't make up its mind. I snuggle under my comforter and open my New York map. What was Ichabod's next stop? His diary says Brutus. I can't find it, even with my magnifying glass. What has happened to all of Ichabod's towns?

9 November 1811
Mr. Phelps in Brutus

I share my Brutus dilemma with Karen the following morning as she serves me cranberry French toast with bacon, strawberries and orange slices, strong coffee, and fresh grapefruit juice. What a contrast to Ichabod's bowl of Indian cornmeal mush. Moments later, she hands me a Web-page printout with a picture of the Brutus Town Hall.

"Take Route 31 north," she says, leaning over my shoulder. "Watch for the intersection of 107; turn west. When you reach Route 72, turn right. You will enter Weedsport. It's about twenty-five miles north of here. Property records are at the Brutus Town Hall on Main Street."

Nothing made sense. Was I working with pieces from two different puzzles? Why would Ichabod go twenty-five miles off the Genesee route, where winding Indian trails were hardly wide enough for a wagon? The journey west—whether undertaken by foot, horseback, wagon, or boat—was slow and arduous.[12]

I check the diary for his daily weather entry. Rain had been falling on him, too. I write down the directions on the printout.

"Thanks, Karen," I say. "At least I have a chance of finding this missing town before moving on."

I have no trouble finding Weedsport. I stop at a hardware store. Sounds of eighteen-wheelers rumble in the distance along the New York Thruway.

"Is there a town called Brutus around here?" I ask a woman at the cash register. "Yes, there is a Brutus," says a bearded man standing behind me. A red flannel shirt covers his generous middle. "Go two blocks past that stoplight out there. It will be on your left."

I travel less than a block when I see a large sign hanging on a pole. It says "Old Brutus Historical Society." I never reach the Town Hall. Serendipity continues to ride shotgun. I arrive on the one morning of the week that the building is open.

Closing the wooden door behind me, I glance at the vintage cases displaying pocket watches with tarnished gold chains, splintered wooden spoons and bowls, white lace caps, arrowheads, and bullets. A mixture of a past that doesn't connect, like a puzzle before the pieces become a picture. A mannequin wearing a long skirt and a high-necked blouse stands in the corner. Black iron cooking pots with stubby legs charred from fire coals line one wall. Moldy odors match the gray drizzle outside. A guest book rests atop a dusty display case. I sign my name.

Voices are coming from a back room. I walk closer and peek into a cramped room lined with large metal filing cabinets and stacks of small cardboard boxes. Three gray-haired women are sitting around a long wooden table. They appear to be cataloging donations. They look up, not the least bit surprised to see a stranger in their midst.

"Hi," I say. "I'm sorry to interrupt you. I was wondering if you had any information on Vermonters migrating west in the early eighteen hundreds. My great-great-great-grandfather Ichabod stopped overnight in Brutus in 1811 on his way to the Holland Purchase lands." The women grin.

"What was his last name? Crane?" asks the one wearing a purple sweat suit. I laugh.

"No, Foster," I say. I tell them about his diary, his stopover in Brutus, and the people with whom he stayed.

"Join us," says Jeanne, their Society president. I pull up a chair, feeling comfortable in their sanctuary of treasured Brutus memorabilia.

"Who did he stay with in Brutus?" asks Helen, a short, round-faced woman with a wide mouth, a flat nose, and straight gray-black hair covering her ears.

"His diary said Mr. Phelps," I say.

Three mouths open in unison. Not a sound comes out. The women slide their chairs, climbing over one another in their rush to grab a painting leaning against the back wall. Vivian gets her hands on it first.

"This picture was donated yesterday," she says, gripping a watercolor of a gray log cabin surrounded by green meadows and tall oak trees. "It's a painting of the cabin where your Ichabod spent the night!" she says. This time it's my mouth that drops open.

Why had I ended up at Hobbit Hollow Farm where Karen initiated an Internet search on Brutus? Why am I sitting around this table with three strangers on the one morning a week they catalog donations? Why had descendants of Ichabod's host family donated the old log cabin painting the day before I arrive? Didn't I already know the answers?

"Being here with you is unplanned, yet someone planned it," I say. "I believe we were meant to meet today."

"This often happens to me with ancestral conversations," Jeanne says. "I went to a Palatine reunion in New Jersey several years ago. When I walked into the sanctuary of the original church where my ancestors worshipped, my hair bristled. I had a quiver rush through my stomach." Jeanne's blues eyes brighten. She holds her stomach. "It was as if they were there, in that church, right there with me."

"I experienced the presence of my ancestors one night in Rutland," I say, describing their faces and black capes. "That image sticks in my memory, like a snapshot in an album."

"Is the cabin still standing?" I ask.

"No, but I know where it was," says a voice behind me. A tall, large-framed man wearing blue jeans, a plaid cotton shirt, and a royal-blue baseball cap shuffles into the room carrying maps.

"This area from Skaneateles to the present New York Thruway over yonder was all Brutus when your Ichabod came through," he says, his jaw set, his eyes all-knowing. He opens a road map on the table. "Brutus isn't really anything more than the Village of Weedsport and some surrounding countryside today," he says. "The Phelps property was at a crossroads near an old cemetery on Franklin Avenue, the old Genesee Road near Skaneateles."

"Meet my husband, Raymond," Jeanne says.

The room buzzes, like bees circling their hive.

"In those days it was all rock, mud, mire, and trees here, you know?" Raymond says.

"Oh, and that oil lamp over there came in with the Phelps picture yesterday," Vivian says. "It might have been in the log cabin that rainy night Ichabod was there."

"Can I copy that page from his diary that mentions Brutus?" Raymond asks. "We'll file it with the Phelps and add the name Foster."

I feel like Johnny Appleseed, dropping pages of Ichabod's life along his trail to Willink, keeping him alive. I photograph Vivian, Helen, Jeanne, and Raymond holding the log cabin painting and the page from Ichabod's diary.

Raymond gives me a map highlighting the country roads leading back to the Phelps property. Rain seeps into my hair as I run to my car. Will it ever stop? I spend the next hour riding on narrow roads that encompass the Brutus of 1811. I stop at the old Phelps corner on Franklin Street. A large, two-story colonial house has replaced the log cabin, but I am thrilled to find an exact place where Ichabod stopped. I look across the fields and try to imagine his wagon parked under a tree. Suddenly, I hear the deafening sound of an air horn. An eighteen-wheeler is barreling down on me. My hands are shaking as he rumbles past in the oncoming lane. My breath collapses into my chest. If I don't focus on where I am, I might not be long among the living.

After Brutus, Ichabod's route became more difficult for him. His most primitive trails lay ahead. Rain or snow socked his wagon nearly every day until he hugged his son Benjamin and his family in their one-room log cabin in Willink on November 28, 1811. I picture his boots sinking into mud, his wagon wheels dragging through the ruts Raymond described, wolves howling when the moon appears, and bears sniffing around the trees. He was alone on the trail, no neighbor to run to if Susannah developed a fever. His next stop is missing on my map, but at least I'm traveling on the old Genesee Trail to Buffalo.

10 November 1811
Mr. Miller at Junius

One main route for settlers led west from here. The road was a widened Indian path with mud holes that covered the hubs of wagon wheels. A few low areas had stretches of "cour-deeroy" logs laid side by side to provide a roadway surface. Flatlands and low rolling hills were densely wooded with oak, maple, hickory, cherry, beech, and sycamore, accented with occasional rocky limestone outcroppings.[13]

The Fosters and their neighbors had been moving west for more than twenty years, going back and forth, checking out the land, and eventually moving permanently.

Newspapers carried advertisements saying New York land was well-timbered, well-watered, easily accessible and undeniably fertile . . . all to be had on long-term payment for only two or three dollars an acre. . . . There were letters from Vermonters already in the West, singing the praises of the new country. Now and then a group of young men set out on a wide ranging tour of a thousand miles or more to discover just how true were all these glowing reports, and usually they came back satisfied and prepared to emigrate permanently.[14]

Ichabod's children followed this pattern. His oldest son, Benjamin; his wife, Lydia; and their six young children had traveled this route five months before Ichabod set out. Benjamin had made numerous trips to western New York before he settled on Willink. Young men often hiked or rode their horses to the country beyond the Genesee.

11 February 1791
Aron Beach and Mr. Sawyer set out with
there familys for Genesees

7 June 1807
Benjamin Carr & Moses Munger came to our house
on their way to the Holland Purchase

11 July 1807
Moses Munger was at our house on his
return home from Lake Eare

27 May 1810
Benj & Gideon Walker set out for Holland Purches

22 October 1810
Thomas Webb came to our house from Welink in the Holland
Purchas

7 January 1811
Mr. Spencer set out for York State

22 February 1811
I heard that Benjamin with his family was seen near to Utica

4 June 1811
Stukeley Stone Esq set out for the Holland Purches

29 June 1811
I received a letter that Benj Foster sent to S. Beach
receiving date June the 5 1811 in which he informed him
of the safe arrival of himself and family in Holland Purchase . . .

Ichabod's sons were patterning their lives after his, leaving settled lands they had cleared, selling out for a profit, seeking cheap farmland. Ichabod had left Rhode Island for Vermont in 1770 for the same reason. His father, Benjamin, at age fifty-four had come along. Ichabod's sons Benjamin, Albro, Samuel, John, and Ichabod Jr. moved to western New York in the early 1800s. Only William appears to have remained in Vermont. When the Fosters started moving west, Whiting and Middletown residents were marketing practically all their extra produce in Canada. Suddenly, this practice ended with President Jefferson's embargo in 1808. Farm prices tumbled. People tried to collect debts when no one had cash.[15] Ichabod left for New York after the 1811 flood destroyed the businesses in Middletown. That same year, the Vermont State Bank, the center of the state's financial system, collapsed.

Then came the War of 1812, which further destabilized the state. By 1813, an epidemic of spotted fever, known today as cerebro-spinal meningitis, swept through the state. Tuberculosis was stalking the hillsides. . . . Consumption, as it was then called, was little understood either as to its cause or its cure. All through Vermont's early history, it accounted for a fourth to a third of the annual death toll. . . . Perhaps the heaviest blow, which hit Vermont in any of those years, was the "cold season" of 1816. On the eighth of June snow fell to a depth of several inches, ice formed on the

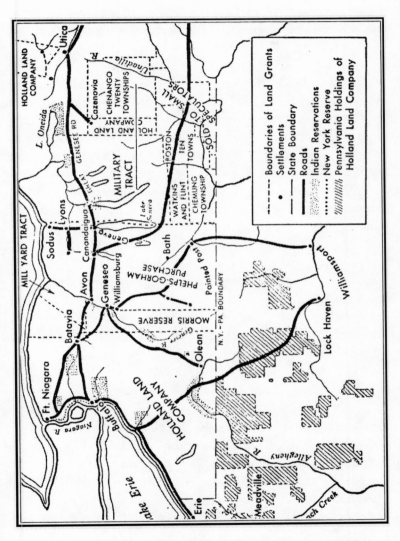

New York and Pennsylvania frontier, 1790–1812

ponds, leaves froze on the trees, and the growing crops throughout the state were almost completely ruined. . . . One reads of families subsisting on hedgehogs, boiled nettles and clover heads.[16]

As long as western and northern New York continued to contain wild lands that were both cheap and tillable, Vermont migration continued. When these lands were exhausted, soon after 1820, the migration stopped.[17]

The last Foster to move was Ichabod's son John, who built a log cabin on Lot 51 next to Benjamin's in 1815, shortly after the War of 1812 ended.

When I leave Brutus, I spend the rest of the day driving through small towns like Lima, Avon, Caledonia, and Stafford.

11 November 1811
Drive Mr. S. Roberts   Seneca

12 November 1811
Lay by

13 November 1811
Drive Mr. Whitney   Gorham

14 November 1811
Drive Mr. Sterling   Lima

15 November 1811
Mr. Davie   Caladonia

I imagine the Fosters each night drying their clothes in front of a friend's hearth or eating venison prepared by a stranger. Some of the names in Ichabod's diary were friends of friends, names given to him before he left Whiting. Some were family. Doors in the wilderness were open to families moving through or coming from far away. James Sterling, who gave Ichabod's family a meal and a place to sleep, Nathaniel Munger, and Samuel Carr were former Vermonters, named in the diary, who helped settle Lima.

These early settlers were mainly of traditional New England stock, sturdy pioneers, who found these hills and vales of the Genesee Valley to their liking. They were not paragons. They were rough men in a rough time, but always they stood on their own feet. They had to, for they faced so many enemies; wild beasts and hostile Indians; they had to conquer the elements, the "Genesee Fever," want, and loneliness.[18]

The road is straight and level. Some communities on the western route, such as Skyler and Sullivan, have exits. Others, such as Gorham, once a large tract, don't appear on the old trail. The land between Geneva and Batavia rose and rounded off with wide views. When Ichabod walked by, most of the land was rough and unbroken. He spent three nights in Batavia before walking the last twelve miles west to Buffalo. Willink's Lot 51 is south of Buffalo along trails not identified on maps of 1810.

16 November 1811
Mr. Peat Batave

17 November 1811
Mr. Richardson Batave

18 November 1811
Mr. S. Carr Batave

My headlights reflect puddles as I enter Batavia. Clouds keep dumping their contents. The continual rain depresses me. I leave the congested streets clogged with bright-orange cones, bulldozers, and heavy trucks full of blacktop. The drizzle that has dragged on all day adds to my dismal opinion of Batavia. I'm glad I have not booked reservations, even though Ichabod stayed here for three nights. As I enter Clarence, the oldest existing town in Erie County, the noise of the New York Thruway closes in, like an approaching freight train.

I stop at the Asa Ransom House, a restored village inn on Route 5, to inquire about a room. In 1799, the Holland Land Company offered lots ten miles apart to "any proper man who would build and operate a tavern upon it." Asa Ransom was among the first to accept this opportunity; and in the hollow of the ledge, near a pine grove, he built a log home, a tavern, and a gristmill.[19]

Joseph Ellicott, the surveyor who laid out lots like Benjamin's throughout the Holland Land Company holdings in western New York, set up his first land office in Ransom's tavern in 1801. His survey was finished in October 1800, and the next month he signed a contract to serve as resident-agent in charge of land sales, a position he held for the next twenty years. Ellicott was described as "short tempered, somewhat tactless with an inner drive that made him rather dictatorial." At six feet three inches tall, he was an imposing figure. He reported that the soil was suitable for raising corn, wheat, rye, and other grains. Rattlesnakes, bears, wolves, elk, foxes, deer, mink, and otters occupied the woods, which were full of sugar maple, beech, oak, ash, and elm.[20]

He thought the company should spend as little money as possible on development such as roads, gristmills, and taverns, thereby adding to the miserable traveling conditions for Ichabod and his family. He also established the terms under which Ichabod's son Benjamin signed his Article of Agreement on Lot 51, the land where the Fosters would settle.

Ichabod didn't stop at the Ransom tavern, but stayed instead with Mr. Sparling.

19 November 1811
Mr. P. Sparling   Clarance

Today the inn is a full-service establishment with a library, a gift shop, and an herb garden. The sign on the door reads, "where time stands still and memories come alive." I ask the innkeeper if he knows of a Sparling family or an old log cabin their ancestors might have built along this route. He shakes his head but suggests I check with the Clarence Historical Society up the street in the morning.

Firelight warms my room at the inn. "For the Beauty of the Earth" drifts over the intercom. I wrap in a terry-cloth robe, sipping tea in bed. I think about my visit to the Brutus Historical Society this morning and feel grateful I touched the Phelps painting and saw the property on Franklin Avenue where the log cabin once stood. If I had planned every stop, every layover along Ichabod's 1811 trail to Willink, I would have focused on each day's destination rather than on the journey with all its intuitive and serendipitous offerings. I feel connected like a fragile yet firm line of a spider's web, weaving my search among my migrating ancestors and America's struggle to expand. Only the perfect center knows where I will end up, but I know why I came on this journey. I had no choice. Someone sent me.

Tomorrow Ichabod and I will travel the last twelve miles to Buffalo and turn south for Willink. This part of the route

between Batavia and Buffalo was said to be one of the worst
mud-rutted stretches, with only a desolate-looking log cabin
here and there the whole way. Did one of his wagon wheels
crack, an ox die, a child get sick? Ichabod's diary mentions
only where they stopped. He never mentions that he stayed
in a tavern or an inn during this long journey. However, his
next two stops could have been taverns, as a Mr. Miller and a
Mr. Leach were known to have operated taverns where travel-
ers would spend the night, according to John Conlin, editor of
Western New York Heritage magazine.

20 November 1811
Mr. Miller   Buffelow

21 November 1811
Mr. Leach   Buffelow

I can't imagine how much dirt clung to his pants or how
many holes cut through his boot leather. Could he survive a
few more days on the trail, carrying visions of grandchildren
hugging his knees? I feel like a cloud, expanding, filling with
anticipation. Will I see his log cabin, his grave? Will I see him
again?

The next morning, I stop at the Clarence Historical Society. A board meeting is in progress. I don't stay. The secretary takes my copy of Ichabod's diary page for Clarence and
places it in a manila folder. "We'll keep this in our archives,"
she says. No one knows of the Sparling log cabin. The chair-
person points to the Goodrich-Landow log cabin, built in the
early part of the 1800s, which is being restored in the side
yard. It could have been Mr. Phelps's home. It resembles the
painting.

Once again, drizzle is edging toward ice on my windshield. I drive the last twelve miles to Buffalo with the sounds of the New York Thruway vibrating in my ears. I turn onto the beltway south to Willink. Our westward trek is ending—his, five weeks; mine, five days.

Chapter Six

THE LAST MILE

I follow the beltway east of Buffalo, avoiding city traffic, and turn south on Route 219 toward Hamburg. Drizzle mixed with snow slides down my windshield, sending chills through my bare hands. The temperature hovers in the low 30s. However, I am drier than Ichabod had been. I imagine him bucking a southwest wind off Lake Erie as snow soaks his britches. This route had been an Iroquois trail when Ichabod traveled the last leg of his long journey from Whiting to Willink. My journey is ending, too.

Will I find his bones buried on his son's property, or will his identity linger only in his written words? One other piece of Ichabod's history, the record of Benjamin's land transaction, is missing. A microfilm copy of his oldest son's original property agreement for Lot 51, issued through Joseph Ellicott, is cataloged in the Reed Library on the campus of the State University of New York in Fredonia along with all the Holland Land Company Records. As with Ichabod's first property indenture, signed in 1761, I long to copy the evidence identifying the last piece of land where he lived. Dutch proprietors Wilhem Willink, Jan Willink, Wilhem Willink the younger, and Jan Willink the younger had acquired more than three million acres in western New York in December 1792 and February and July 1793 from Robert Morris, who had purchased the property from Massachusetts in May 1791. The original records remain in Holland.

After a short drive, I check into the Colonial Retreat Bed and Breakfast in Hamburg, and ask the innkeeper for the shortest route to Fredonia. "Take the New York Thruway," she says. I pause, remembering my vow not to travel on major highways. Ichabod never went to Fredonia. His route veered southeast after Hamburg. I justify my detour, knowing I'll be back on his trail in the morning. Soon my speedometer hits sixty-five for the first time since I left Coventry, Rhode Island, the beginning point of Ichabod's trail.

Heavy white flakes cling to my jacket as I walk through the main entrance to the Reed Library an hour later. I ask the receptionist how to find Benjamin Foster's land records.

"Our archivist, Jack Ericson, can help you," she says. "He's in today. He usually isn't. Don't be intimidated by him. He's a gruff, belligerent man. Just bark back."

"Thanks for the tip," I say. She directs me through an atrium arch, a warm, renewing space. I turn right. At the end of the hall, I enter a room lined with shelves of old books and a center table crowded between stacks of card files. In the far corner, circular steps lead to an upstairs room. A pencil holder competes for breathing room on a desk smothered in paper. Manila files lean on each other. Does Mr. Ericson work around this pile of apparent confusion? He's the curator of the Holland Purchase Land Company collection.

Two women are thumbing through cards on the table. "Mr. Ericson is attending a meeting," one woman says. "I doubt he will have time for you."

I return to the main library, feeling lost, not sure where to go next. I notice a microfilm room lined with machines, file drawers, and several tables. The room is still. I breathe deeply, trying to collect my thoughts. The Holland Land

Company records are massive. Benjamin was one of hundreds of settlers "articled" property in more than three million acres. The Company seldom deeded land directly. Ichabod's son signed Articles of Agreement that outlined the terms under which he would eventually purchase his land. The terms varied and were often adjusted by the agent as he saw fit. Generally, a down payment was required, interest terms agreed to, and a time limit for payment specified, usually eight to ten years. Deeds weren't given until the account was paid in full.[1]

I hear an irritated voice behind me saying, "I was told you wanted to see me."

I turn. Staring at me through rimless glasses is a husky man, round in the middle, with white short-cropped hair and a face to match his roundness.

"Yes. How do I find the microfilm for Range 7, Section 6, Lot 51? I'm looking for the land record for Benjamin Foster. I located these numbers in Karen Livsey's book on the Holland Land Company."

"Did you read her introduction?" he asks.

"Yes."

"Well, most people don't," he says. " Where did you find the book?"

"At the New-York Historical Society library several years ago," I say, trying to sound professional. I wasn't sure where all this was leading, but I didn't want to lose him.

Mr. Ericson walks over to a series of drawers lining a long wall, and pulls out the book he thinks I need. He tosses it on the table and walks out.

"Thank you," I say. I don't think he heard me.

The book lists information I already had. I walk back through the atrium to Mr. Ericson's office, hoping he hasn't disappeared.

"You're lazy," he shouts from behind his desk. "You want to be spoon-fed."

I'm grateful the librarian had warned me about his communication style. I can't see a smile line around his mouth.

He turns away and climbs the circular stairs to his apparently private collection. When he returns, he has a thin yellow file tucked under his arm.

"Why are you doing this?" he asks. "Genealogy, I suppose."

"No. I understand where Benjamin fits in my family. I'm looking for details that will add color to a book which will end on Lot 51."

I feel his persona lighten. Does he think I'm an academic, a writer, a curious scholar? He slips into his chair, leans back, and slides the file across the papers on his desk. I catch it before it hits the floor. It contains a small index book describing more than two hundred microfilm reels. I sit at the table across from his desk. There are no titles like "article" or "land" or any alphabetical listing of settlers. I'm not interested in correspondence between Joseph Ellicott and his subagents. I don't see the name Benjamin Foster anywhere. I feel my energy waning. My eyelids droop.

Benjamin was one of hundreds of pioneers with no money, only hope for a better life. Mr. Ellicott needed these early pioneers to clear and settle the land so it would grow in value. He thought sales would be easy but collections difficult, so he accepted payments in cattle, hogs, and grain. He knew many pioneers, such as Benjamin, would purchase small lots of about 120 acres at about two dollars and fifty cents per acre and would clear the land for farming.

How did these pioneers earn cash to pay for their articled land? Their crops fed their families or served as barter for nails or leather or iron. Who had extra crops to sell? If they did, who had money to purchase the corn or wheat? It was difficult to meet cash payment schedules.[2]

The agents tended to be lenient in the collection of payments if the settler was living and working on his purchase. Benjamin had exchanged the rocky Vermont soil for muddy, rich, black dirt that seemed either to remain wet or to be buried under a foot of snow. I imagine the wind off Lake Erie, rumbling like a freight train, burrowing down on his family's log cabin in winter. At least firewood was plentiful.

I page through the index again, hoping to find something relevant. I notice Mr. Ericson is reading an article. He pauses.

"You still want to be spoon-fed?" he asks.

"I can't find what I'm looking for," I say. "Maybe I don't know how to explain it to you."

He climbs his circular staircase again and returns with a new volume on the Holland Purchase history. This reference adds a dab of color to the stark details of land purchase. I discover the price nearly doubled after Benjamin received his article in 1810. Although agents tried to charge more, they considered taking in-kind for principal payments. However, nothing here leads to Benjamin's land agreement. I sense Mr. Ericson knows this and is baiting me. I hold on to my line of silence, staring down at the smooth table. His hand holds the rod and reel. I look up, pleading with my eyes for him to hook the right index listing. He slides his chair back, pushes his pencil down hard on the paper he was reading, and lumbers back up the stairs. He returns with another thin folder. Why didn't he bring all the files the first time?

"Write these numbers down," he says. "Reel 3 H65H64H654, Erie County Land Records. They should tell you about his land."

His lips curl up. Slightly. Is there a heart of kindness beating underneath this gruff exterior? I thank him and rush back to the microfilm room.

I find the drawer, locate reels 8 and 9 for Range 7, but not reel 3. I slink back to the office, feeling small and stupid. He glares at me through his rimless glasses, gets up, and walks me to the microfilm room, like a principal marching a child to his office for disciplinary action.

"You didn't pull the drawer out far enough," he says, grabbing the right reel. "Here, put this in the microfilm machine over there." He walks out. I don't blame him for being aggravated with me. I'm irritated with myself, too.

I slide the feeder film under the glass, attaching it to the reel. Next, I push the forward knob. No index appears. The first tattered pages have lost their legible numbers. I hit fast-forward in frustration. The reel is clattering like a Model T speeding down a gravel road. I let it roll. I don't know why. The reel is out of control. So am I. I lift my hand. The machine rests in quiet anticipation as the script comes into focus. Is it a mirage? Who controlled the fast-forward button? The ladies of the Brutus Historical Society would probably say it's all Ichabod's doing. The name Benjamin C. Foster appears across the top of the page.

The script is faint, but legible. Benjamin was articled 256 acres. He deposited $18 on May 3, 1810, for a piece of land priced at $576. He agreed to clear the land, plant crops, and build a dwelling house within five years, and pay off his principal within ten. No deed would pass to him until his principal was paid in full. If he failed, the Holland Land Company would repossess his property. He was expected to make regular payments or lose his land.[3] He returned to Vermont and prepared to move his wife and children the following year.

29 June 1811

I received a letter that Benj Foster sent to S. Beach [his wife's father] receiving date June the 5th 1811 in which he informed him of the safe arrival of him self and family in Holland Purchase . . .

Gently, I move the reel forward. In 1813, he deferred his first interest payment of ten dollars. His son-in-law, Stukely Stone, paid an accumulated fifty dollars interest payment for him on May 23, 1813. By May 1818, a neighbor, Johnathan Townsend, took over 152 acres of Lot 51. A man whose name I can't read purchased or articled the rest. Later, the Stanbro family purchased Benjamin's land and received the first fully paid deed for the property in 1834 from Wilhem Willink.[4]

I sink back in my chair. Sadness smothers my enthusiasm, like a wet blanket tossed over a warm fire. Benjamin lost his land before he could acquire title to it. Why did he miss his interest payments? Was it because of his sadness? His wife, Lydia, had died in 1816, apparently in childbirth. He took her body back to her birthplace in Whiting, where her gravestone stands next to the gravestone of her parents, Samuel and Mary Beach, in the yard behind the old Community Church. His two-year-old daughter died in Willink in 1818.

These first settlers were for the most part poor. They had few facilities for making any labor light, their whole existence was a battle against hardship. The wolves took their sheep, there were few body comforts, prices were so high that they made all luxuries prohibitive. There was little social life and the few churches and schools were of the crudest type.[5]

Should I tell Mr. Ericson how I found Benjamin's records among the hundreds on the reel? Would he believe me? I keep the pages on the screen and rush to his office. He isn't there. The room is empty. I write a thank-you note and balance it against the files on his desk. As I turn to leave, I hear slow, methodical footsteps coming down the wooden stairs. Does he ever let anyone follow him up there to see what he has stashed away?

"I found Benjamin's record for Lot 51 on the microfilm," I say. He says nothing. He reaches his desk and picks up my note. Smile lines appear. Have we reached common ground?

"Say, now that I know your last name, you should research the Van Camps. They were plentiful around here."

"Good idea," I say. "I'll save that for another visit. I'm heading for Lot 51 now."

We walk to the microfilm room. He prints the Foster pages and slips them into a file folder for me.

"I'd like to see your book when it's finished," he says.

"I'll send you a draft."

"Why did you come into work today?" I ask. "I was told this wasn't your day to be here."

"I don't know," he says. "I just did."

We shake hands. Mr. Ericson shuffles back to his office. The receptionist watches as he passes through the atrium.

"I didn't need to bark back," I say to her. "He actually smiled."

"Good," she says. "Did you find what you were looking for?"

"Yes, I found Benjamin Foster's Articles of Agreement and the history of his involvement with the property. Thanks for your advice."

I slip my new file into my backpack as the receptionist carefully removes the reel and returns it to the right drawer.

❧

I return to Hamburg. Soft snowflakes block what remains of the day's light as I park at The Common Ground, a restaurant recommended by my innkeeper. I enter a quiet space. Apple basket lampshades reflect yellow light across the dining area. Barn beams and siding form the interior walls. A mural of the sun rising over waves with a quotation from Revelation covers most of one wall. The twelve tribes complete an arc across the top.

What would Ichabod think? Would he add his own verse to the mural? He hadn't mentioned his Bible for two years and never noted reading chapters or verses during his life in western New York. Why he stopped remains a mystery. Perhaps because no Baptist congregation gathered near the family's log cabin.

"What brings you to Hamburg?" asks a soft-spoken man with a tiny ponytail and a short gray beard as he guides me to a table.

"I couldn't find lodging in the town of Concord [formerly Willink] where my great-great-great-grandfather died in 1813. Besides, I want to explore an old mill here in Hamburg where his sons carried the family's corn to be ground. Late this afternoon I discovered a strong creek, almost a small river, near my bed and breakfast on Main Street," I say. "Could that be Eighteen Mile Creek? I know it runs through Hamburg."

"Probably is," he says. "But I don't know about an old mill."

A moment later, he sets a steaming bowl of vegetable soup on my table.

"What kind of mill?" he asks.

"I think a gristmill."

He disappears behind a nearby booth. I can't see to whom he is talking.

"Yes, remains of an old gristmill are just below the falls," he says, handing me a diagram drawn on the back of a meal receipt. "The man at that next booth told me."

I walk over to thank him.

"I assume you're the one who drew this diagram," I say.

"Yes, I'm an environmentalist studying water flow in the area," he says. "You should be able to find the remains of the mill. Be careful. It's steep and can be treacherous going under the bridge."

Thanks for your help," I say. "If you and I hadn't been dining at The Common Ground at the same time, I doubt if I would've found anyone with knowledge of the old mill."

❧

The next morning, my watch reads five minutes to eight when I park near a concrete bridge, high above Eighteen Mile Creek. The gravel shoulder is damp. I crawl under the bridge, bracing my body with my right arm, and slide down a steep, slippery bank of scree. For twenty minutes, I creep along the edge of the creek, crushing autumn castoffs under my feet, now and then tossing one into the flow, watching it meander softly out of sight.

I notice a pile of gray boards up ahead, some leaning against one another, some tangled on the ground, others stretching over the water. Across the shallow creek stands a crumbling lime-green and black wall of stone. Slow, cascading falls churn between.

The creek bottom looks surreal, like slate laid down to smooth the way for the water. Had Ichabod looked at these same falls, walked along this same shore? Could this be the spot where the Foster corn was ground into samp for the family's breakfast? Is this the remains of the mill mentioned in Ichabod's diary? I want to believe it is. No signs say otherwise. John Cummings had erected a gristmill here in 1806.

25 January 1812
Benj'n and Sam'll went to Eighteen mile Creek

12 February 1812
Benj set out for Eighteen mile Creek and returned on 13

3 March 1812
Benj set out for Eighteen mile Creek

1 April 1812
Benj went to mill and got 17 bushels of corn
ground and brought it home

I linger, listening to the water pass, picturing Ichabod's sons delivering the family's corn to Mr. Cummings. Ichabod never again mentioned Eighteen Mile Creek except to say that British troops raided homes along the creek several months later, during the War of 1812. I feel that same gentle connection floating in the greenish-gray bottom, lacing me to my ancestors. No images appear. However, after my wild ride with the microfilm machine yesterday, nothing surprises me anymore.

Ichabod was seventy-two at the time, and appears to have devoted his energy to planting cabbage and turnips, potatoes and carrots, grapevines and cherry trees in Willink.

21 March 1812
I set my grape veins and barberry seeds into dirt

27 April 1812
I soe cabage parsnips and turnip seed

I walk back under the bridge. If I attempt to climb up the way I slid down, I'll have no traction. I follow the stream below the bridge, noticing a patch of brush and straggly maple trees covered with tangled vines. I dig my boots into the bank, slipping, grabbing vines, jamming my knees into the dirt.

Mud clogs my fingernails as I push with my toes and pull with
my hands. Finally, I drag myself over the edge. I'm lying in
a large pasture not far from the road. Why was this side trip
necessary? Do I need to touch and see all that might remain of
Ichabod's life to feel authentic in my search for him?

I climb back into my car and head south. My windshield
wipers slap back and forth as I enter the farmland and forests of
Erie County. I notice oak trees along the Boston–West Springville Road struggling to hang on to their few remaining leaves.
Winter is approaching. Ichabod would have watched for wolves
and bears in the brush. I picture him trudging through snow,
flakes melting on his white beard, his boots soaked through
to his socks, his chin tucked from the wind. Susannah and
little Susanna huddle under blankets, hiding their faces from
the blustery wind and circling snow as the oxen pull them the
last mile.

22 November 1811
Mr. Brink Willink

23 November 1811
Mr. Right Willink

24 November 1811
Esqr Stone Willink

25 November 1811
Lay by at Esqr Stones

26 November 1811
Lay by at Esqr Stones

27 November 1811
Esqr Yaws

It rained or snowed on every one of their final days during the five weeks they spent along the Mohawk to the Genesee and Iroquois trails. Only three times in nearly thirty years of recording weather, births, and visits had Ichabod written about traveling with his wife. I imagine they witnessed each other's courage and patience, stamina and prayers, along with their moans, cries, and longings to return to Vermont. They didn't turn back. They kept pushing west. Ichabod thanked God for their safe arrival at Benjamin's cabin in Willink.

28 November 1811
To B.C. Fosters in Willink where we arrived in safly through the Divine Goodness which completed a journey of 5 weeks

Today, will anyone know where Lot 51 is? I notice a sign saying, "Concord, organized on March 20, 1812." When the Fosters arrived, this large area was called Willink, after the Holland Land Company proprietors. Today, it is broken into numerous towns and villages. My speedometer reads 589 miles. I had clicked it to zero when I left Ichabod's farmhouse in Whiting.

Snowflakes slide down my windows as I turn onto Genesee Road. Rolling farmland edged with maple and oak melts into the horizon. Somewhere in that soil stretching before me Ichabod's bones may still rest. I notice Townsend Road, perhaps named for the one who secured part of Benjamin's property when he couldn't pay the interest. Could Lot 51 be nearby? I enter the village of Springville in the town of Concord. On the side of the road is a historical sign. It reads:

First Settler Town of Concord
Christopher Stone, in 1807, for $1575
bought 787 acres of land in this area,
including some of the village of

Springville. His was the first settlement
on this site. His son, Lucius, was the
first white child born, in 1809,
in the town of Concord, N.Y.
Whence Stone came or whither he went is an
unsolved mystery.

Ichabod's diary solves the first part of that mystery. Christopher appears in the diary when the Fosters lived in Whiting.

23 April 1804
Christopher Stone came to our house

I believe his mother married Ichabod's youngest brother, Joel, making us kin as well. Could the restored log cabin in back be the one where Ichabod stayed during the "lay by" for three nights with Esquire Stone? Margaret Mayerat, the Concord historian, will know. She is expecting me. I spot her office sign in the next block. The thermometer on the nearby bank building hovers around freezing. Frosty gusts wrap around my ears as I knock. Margaret opens the glass door, her white hair curled from a fresh perm. She is dressed in a blue sweatshirt and black slacks.

"Well, what do you want to know?" she says. "Sit down. Let's talk. I think we can find Lot 51, but it has been broken up many times since Benjamin's day." She rolls with enthusiasm, like the Energizer bunny. I'm grateful to meet another primary source person like Karen in Rhode Island and Grace in Vermont. Margaret is dedicated to preserving her local history and eager to hear what Ichabod wrote in his diary. We sit at a long table. I lay out the Willink pages that tell about his life in Concord in 1811 and 1812.

10 January 1812
I made the first basket in Willink

22 February 1812
Sam'll had a daughter born in the night

As fast as I read one page, she races to her copy machine in a side room.

"I'm glad another historical society will treasure his writings," I say.

"Oh my, yes. Look at all these names of people he knew who appear in Erasmus Briggs's *History of Concord*.[6] I can start a Foster file now," Margaret says as she unlocks a glass cupboard lined with books, their bindings cracking.

"You need to read what Mr. Briggs has to say about life in those days, and especially about your family," she says, handing me the one published piece of evidence confirming that my family lived here. Margaret turns to page 368. She reads aloud:

Benjamin C. Foster came and located on lot fifty-one, township seven, range six before the war of 1812 and was the first on that lot; he set out the orchard that still stands a short distance up the side-hill on the old Amos Stanbro place, and there is where his log house was located. His children were Otis, Susan, who married Stukely Stone, Polly, Adaline, Lucy, Delia, Benjamin and Samuel.

Benjamin C. Foster and Stukely Stone went from this town to Cambria, Niagara county, sixty years ago [1823], and finally to Hume, Allegany county.[7]

"You know Briggs charged you to have your family in his book," Margaret says. "If you didn't pay, you weren't in it."

She makes me wonder who paid for the two Foster listings when the book was published in 1883. Below Benjamin's information appears that of his brother John.

Margaret continues reading:

John S. Foster, brother of Benjamin C., came here after the close of the war [of 1812] and built him a house beside his brother's on the same lot and remained a few years and then removed to Hartland, Niagara county, where he died. His children were:

Freelove, who married Whitman Stone.
Lovica, who married Levi Palmer.
Sally, who married Ephraim Needham,
and now resides in Brant.
Amanda, who married Uriah Chapel
and lives in Kendall county, Ill.
John S. lives in Brant.
George W. lives in Elkhart, Ind.
Amy and Alma, dead.[8]

"Margaret, the snow is sticking to the sidewalk. Do you get a lot of it here?" I ask.

"You better believe we do," she says. "The storms blow in off Lake Erie, and as the pressure rises, the hill blocks the winds and all the snow falls here before the storm moves east. More than once, I've slept under my desk in the old Hotel Statler when it snowed too much for me to get home."

"What kind of individuals would risk pneumonia and death, animal attacks, and endure months of stormy weather

in unsettled Willink?" I ask.   "There weren't even any schools
or churches when Ichabod arrived."

Margaret hands me Mr. Briggs's book, opened to page 100.
"Read this for your answer," she says. I read to her this time.

*As a rule, the pioneers of the Holland Purchase were men
of splendid physique, intelligent, self-reliant and possessed great
strength, courage and endurance, which stood them well in hand
in the herculean task they had in rescuing this fair domain from
a savage state. They came of noble race and could trace their lineage back to the pilgrims who landed on Plymouth rock, through
the bloody times that tried men's souls during the dark days of the
Revolution. . . . They had left the homes and scenes of their childhood and bid good-bye to early associates and friends, turned their
faces toward the setting sun, and with their wives and little ones
had started forth on their long and weary journey towards their
future homes. . . . When they at last arrived at their destination,
within the dense forests of the Holland Purchase, hundred of miles
away from any city or large village, and without post offices or mail
to aid them in communicating with their Eastern friends, they
selected lands and built their log cabins, without lumber or nails,
and entered upon a new mode of life.*[9]

"It sounds grim," I say as I set the book down on the table.
"My family could have been Erasmus Briggs's model. Margaret, have I told you that Ichabod's great-great-grandfather,
John Foster, arrived in Massachusetts shortly after the Pilgrims
landed on Plymouth Rock? His grandfather was a major during the King Phillips wars, and his father fought in the first war
against Great Britain. When Ichabod arrived in old Willink,
only a few months would pass before guns started firing in the
second war with Great Britain. Several of his sons joined the
New York militia."

"That's quite a family history," Margaret says. "How much will you include in your book?"

"Only Ichabod, since his diary reveals so much about his life as a father, farmer, and inquisitive common man."

After Benjamin built a shelter on Lot 51, he cleared a small plot to plant corn and potatoes and sow turnips. The Fosters were repeating what they had done one generation before, when they came to Vermont, and generations before that, when they settled in Rhode Island and Massachusetts. This pattern continued until Azariah Foster, Ichabod's grandson, started planting corn in Washington County, Iowa, a few months before Confederate guns fired on Fort Sumter.

Margaret and I continue to thumb through Briggs's descriptions of early times in Concord.

New-comers were always warmly welcomed by their predecessors, partly, doubtless, from motives of kindness, and partly because each new arrival helped to redeem the forest from its forbidding loneliness and add to the value of improvements already made. If there were already a few settlers in the locality, the emigrant's family was sheltered by one of them until notice could be given to a log raising.[10]

Ichabod's diary confirmed Briggs's observations.

22 March 1812
Seneca Baker came to Mr. Drakes with his wife and goods

15 April 1812
Sam'll moved his family from Mr. Durhams

25 June 1812
Benjamin raised his house

20 July 1812
Sam'll covered the north side of the roof of the house

27 July 1812
we began to clear land west of the house

Logs were eight to eighteen inches in diameter and ranged from twelve to twenty feet in length. A builder had to find a dozen or more able-bodied men to help him put up his house; and he had to scour the country for many miles to obtain that number. Cracks between the logs were generally chinked up with three-cornered pieces of timber, split out of small basswood trees, fitted in, and plastered with mud both outside and inside. Sometimes the cracks between the logs would be closed up with moss gathered in the woods.[11]

The log cabins were put up without lumber or nails. The logs were cut in advance and drawn to the desired spot by oxen, and four of the largest logs were selected for the bottom layer.[12] Most of the earliest roofs were made of elm or other kinds of bark, laid rough side up and held in place by the weight of poles resting on top and running lengthwise with the roof. A place for a door was sawed out and another for a window. Floors were made of "puncheons" (a split basswood log with a face smoothed) and hewed down with a narrow ax. Chimneys were made of stone, wood, and mud.[13]

I can't imagine how dark these cabins must have been, but Briggs painted a picture in which I could envision the Fosters eating their harvest and sleeping huddled together on makeshift beds. Ichabod planted crops and recorded his daily activities in Concord as he had for more than forty years in Vermont.

12 May 1812
I soed lettace

23 May 1812
I set sage roots

28 May 1812
we planted peach plumbe and cherey stone

27 June 1812
I made Ichabod shoes

29 June 1812
Br. Joel was at our house

27 September 1812
I finished writing a number of letters to our friends in Whiting

Seven months after Ichabod arrived in Willink, he recorded the arrival of an express rider delivering President James Madison's proclamation of war against Great Britain. These riders spread the news from settlement to settlement in western New York. In late June 1812, fewer than one thousand armed men were available to meet the trained British army across the Niagara River.

28 June 1812
we heard of war being Declared against Greate Britain

31 July 1812
. . . the alarm of war was over Declaration of War
between the United States & Great Britain

In settlements such as these, people had to decide whether to race inland to safety or stay and fight, a situation faced years earlier by the Fosters during the Revolutionary War in Vermont. I picture fear and confusion in the eyes of teenagers as they watch their parents clutching babies on their laps and grandparents sitting around cramped tables sipping coffee in their log cabins as the war news arrived. For Ichabod and his brother Joel, it must have felt like the Revolutionary War starting all over again. Same enemy. Same dismal military conditions. Same frontier situation. The Fosters were living on the outer edges of America when the first shots were fired in northern Vermont, and in western New York when the shooting started once again. War wrapped around their lives, like the cover of a book, holding them captive.

This conflict, often called "Mr. Madison's War," was fueled by the War Hawks in Congress, led by Henry Clay of Kentucky, John C. Calhoun of South Carolina, and William Henry Harrison, governor of the Indiana Territory. The War Hawks pushed for westward expansion, which meant that the Native Americans had to be subdued. Tecumseh, a Shawnee whose name means "panther lying in wait," was resisting any more white settlers moving into the Northwest Territory.

Harrison was intent on removing First Nations people of the Old Northwest to make way for American settlers. His men plundered and burned the Shawnee settlements on November 7, 1811, the day Ichabod stopped in Anadoga en route to Willink. I imagine him walking along the side of his ox-drawn wagon near central New York when Harrison's men attacked.

7 November 1811
drove to Mr. D Gray in Anadoga

Tecumseh was traveling in the South, seeking aid for his cause to unite native tribes and rid his ancestral lands of white occupation. That day, Shawnee homes and food supplies were destroyed during the Battle of Tippecanoe. The following day, Ichabod stopped in Marcellus with the Beach family.

8 November 1811
Marcellus   Mr. Beach

The Indians were so incensed by Harrison's tactics that they joined forces with the British to fight against their common enemy. At the same time, the British had violated American neutral rights by acts of impressment, blockades, and ship seizures, especially on the high seas, where they boarded the ships and captured American seamen, pressing them into service in the British navy. The people with New England and New York shipping and commercial interests were most directly affected by the neutral-rights violations and strongly opposed the war. They disliked losing ships to the British, but realized that war would completely shut down commerce.[14]

Did Ichabod know his youngest son, Albro, my great-great-grandfather, had volunteered for militia duty north of Willink in Jefferson County on July 7, 1812? He enlisted at Sacket's Harbor on the eastern end of Lake Ontario. Albro was a private. That day, Ichabod was busy in his fields.

7 July 1812
We began to set tobaco

According to the New York Index of War Claims, Albro served in the artillery company of the New York militia commanded by Captain Oliver Scott, attached to a regiment of infantry commanded by Colonel Allen, as follows from about the 10th day of July, 1812, to the 24th of the same month, two weeks; from on or about the 7th day of September, 1812, to the 21st of the same month, two weeks; from on or about the 15th of October 1812 to the 15th of November.[15]

He continued to serve until August 1814. His pay for the two weeks in July was two dollars and sixty-six cents,[16] the same for his service in September.[17]

The government order went out to assemble a militia; within a month, three thousand Americans were ready to protect western New York. Accounts say they were poorly trained and ill equipped. Ichabod's other sons must have volunteered. The law of the State of New York from 1776 until some time after the close of the War of 1812 (in June 1815) made it compulsory for every able-bodied male between the ages of eighteen and forty-five to do military duty.[18] This law was strictly enforced, service evaded only by some temporary sickness.[19] Consequently, Ichabod Jr., Samuel, and Benjamin would have been called. Ichabod and his brother Joel were too old.

One of the first major battles of the war was fought at Fort Detroit. The British begin an artillery barrage of the fort on August 15, 1812, after General William Hull refused to surrender. The next morning Native war cries filled the air and had a devastating effect on Hull, Governor of Michigan since 1805. His state of mind quickly deteriorated. He is terrified of being attacked by Tecumseh's tribesmen. His worst nightmare came true as five hundred warriors crossed the Detroit River under the cover of darkness and surrounded the fort. Hull's mind reeling with visions of a bloody massacre of soldiers and civilians, he surrendered despite vehement disagreement from his officers and troops. Hull was certainly not a figure to inspire confidence. Looking far older than his fifty-eight years, he was fat and soft spoken with an annoying habit of chewing tobacco, which, when he was nervous, dribbled down his chin and left stains all over his uniform.[20]

During this period, Ichabod's writings focused mostly on the weather, with no mention of friends visiting.

15 August 1812
sogg morning and misty

17 August 1812
thunder and rain. We began to reepe our wheate

The British took Fort Detroit without a fight. General Isaac Brock, administrator of upper Canada since October 1811, became a hero throughout the British Empire when news arrived that his army had secured a windfall of bounty and supplies.

Accompanied by General Hull, the regulars were marched off to captivity in Quebec while the militia were released on parole. Besides the tremendous loss of materiel that had supplied the poorly equipped Canadian militia, the once-neutral northwest tribes now went over to the British.[21]

30 August 1812
This morning I saw a hand bill that gave an account of
General Hull conduct in surrender of Detroit and
the surrender of his command.

After Hull's defeat, Major General Stephen Van Rensselaer of the New York militia was chosen commander for the Niagara frontier. He picked his nephew and aide-de-camp, Lieutenant Colonel Solomon Van Rensselaer, to lead an attack across the Niagara River. He crossed at Lewistown. The British were camped at Queenston on the opposite side.

a draught of men to garde the lines the 12 of Sept

14 September 1812
the British crose the lake and plunder three
houses on Eighteen Mile Creek. . . .

7 October 1812
. . . 4 o'clock in the morning we hear the firing of cannon

10 October 1812
Sam'll set out for Buffelow on the 7th and returned on the 10th

Was this a militia call-up for Samuel? Why else would he go to Buffalo when cannon and musket fire were flying overhead? On October 13, Van Rensselaer captured the British fort.

October 1812
12 & 13 we here the cannon in Buffelow

British reinforcements arrived. Van Rensselaer hastened back to the American side to bring over more troops, but his men refused to obey his orders. The militia couldn't be ordered out of the state without their consent.

The Americans were attacked and defeated on their own soil. All who had crossed to the Canadian side were killed or captured.[22]

16 October 1812
in the morning we heard of the defeat of our troops in Canada

Morale was low. The troops had camped outside Lewiston since August and hadn't been paid in months. Many of them were missing the harvest on their farms, and lacked food, weapons, and adequate clothing, including shoes. More than half of Van Rensselaer's men, including Ichabod's sons, were militia who were called up for the crisis of the moment but had to return quickly to their farms or face financial ruin.

23 October 1812
We begin to gather our corn

Ichabod's son Albro documented the cost of providing his own clothing and was reimbursed years later. To replace clothing and equipment, he received ninety-five dollars, which was a large sum considering his pay for active service had been about one dollar per week. His claims were not for services but for "contingent expenses"; soldiers in some instances furnished their own transportation as well as their own food and clothing.[23]

With both Generals Hull and Van Rensselaer defeated, Brigadier General Alexander Smyth took over command on the western frontier. He began concentrating troops at Buffalo and Black Rock, preparing to invade Canada. On November 27, 4,500 troops rendezvoused at Black Rock. Smyth would attempt to cross the Niagara River as Van Rensselaer had at Queenston. Orders were issued the next day, but because a large portion of his men were militia, it's not certain how many he could depend on to enter Canada.

28 Nov 1812
we heard cannon all day

Cold sheets of rain drenched the troops waiting to board the boats.

The horrible tempest that had raged for the past twenty-eight hours augured unfavorably for the American venture. The army at Black Rock boarded and reboarded the transports several times in the course of four days, but never left the shore.[24]

Between November 28 and December 1, Brigadier General Smyth failed to reach the Canadian shore. At the same time, Ichabod appeared to be running out of food.

30 November 1812
Mr Durham promised me a bushel of white potatos and
Mr. Drake promise me some corn

After Brigadier General Smyth failed to gain any victories, the army went into winter quarters. With the arrival of harsh weather, poor sanitation conditions, and a lack of provisions and warm clothing, the troops were demoralized. Many had only summer linen uniforms, no blankets, coats, socks, or boots. Food was scarce; and when it did arrive, it was often spoiled.

They were obliged to mount guard during the cold and stormy nights barefooted in their linen jackets and overalls. They are mere militia, and if possible even worse, and if taken into action in their present state would prove more dangerous to themselves than to their enemy.[25]

Ichabod was preoccupied with the weather throughout the battles in November and December. Every day, it snowed or rained.

17 November 1812
the snow fell more than 10 inches

5 December 1812
the snow fell all night

Disease was as bad as a plague among the troops. Militia-men complained of headaches and then in an hour or two were dead. William Hodges was pressed into service making coffins for the deceased. He reportedly made three hundred coffins during the winter of 1812–1813. Dr. Daniel Chapin offered land on his farm for burial. However, much of the ground was rocky; so the graves often were no more than one foot deep. In the spring of 1813, the bodies were exhumed and reburied in a meadow where the ground was sandy and easily dug. Surgeons who attended the wounded and sick complained of the lack of medicine and instruments. Soldiers suffered from typhoid, pleurisy, dysentery, and measles.[26]

Did Samuel or Ichabod Jr. or Benjamin return home sick after fulfilling their required militia service? Could pleurisy, dysentery, or measles have been the cause of four deaths in the Foster log cabin in ten days that December? Four bodies would have been carried from Benjamin's cabin before the sun had set on New Year's Day 1813 and would have been stored somewhere away from wolves until the ground thawed in the spring.

"You better get moving if you're going to hike around Lot 51 before the weather gets worse," Margaret says. "Here, take this map. I've marked the location and the cross roads."

I know that Genesee Road and the old Boston–Springville Road, the ones I had arrived on, cross the Foster land.

"Let me call Doris Biscup to ask if she minds if you walk on her land," Margaret says. "She and her husband built a large log home on Benjamin's hill overlooking his fields." Margaret believes that Ichabod's cabin would have been situated below the old orchard on the hill.

Flurries swirl to the ground, melting in the mud as I walk up an old logging road behind the Biscup home. Will I spot ruins of a cabin, a toppled grave marker, a pile of foundation stones? Will I stumble over the decaying trunks of Ichabod's apple orchard as I search for signs of his grave?

I sit on a damp log on Lot 51, pulling my cap down over my ears, slipping my fingers into my pockets. Flakes fall in no particular direction, landing lightly on my muddy boots. No one makes a sound, not even a sparrow. Gray light will slip soon into dusk and darkness. I have reached the end of my journey. I'm tired. I doubt that I could have endured what Ichabod did—five weeks walking over ruts and roots, through mud, rain, snow, and freezing winds, traveling nearly six hundred miles, at age seventy-two.

Margaret hadn't encouraged me to search for his grave. Too much time has passed, she had said. I don't know if I'm near the old cabin site. Benjamin's original land covered more than two hundred acres.

I notice an old orchard, trunks gnarled, some twisted on the ground. Could this be Ichabod's orchard?

1812
May the 28 we planted peach, plumbe and cherey . . . the east row is late . . . plumbe the north end of the west row . . .

I listen for my soul to tell me what happened nearly two hundred years ago. Ichabod's last diary entry was made on December 27, 1812. His last word on weather is "snow." All month he recorded wind direction, usually SW or W, which meant that the icy gusts from Lake Erie were hitting the logs, howling through the cracks. Snow fell almost every day in December. I picture Ichabod stepping outside to measure the amount.

Ichabod's woods on Lot 51

1 & 2 December 1812
Snow fell 2 inches

5, 6 & 7 December 1812
Snow fell 6 inches

9, 10 December 1812
snow fell

Then a huge storm dumped twenty-two inches in two days.

11 & 12 December 1812
snow fell 22 inches

13 & 14 December 1812
Snow fell 2 inches

17 December 1812
snow in the night 2 inches

Had his son Samuel contracted pneumonia or dysentery during his service with the ill-equipped New York militia in Buffalo before the troops went into winter quarters? Did it spread?

18 December 1812
In the night Sam'll was taken poorly

That day, Ichabod didn't note the snowfall or other weather conditions. Nor did he the next day when he wrote:

19 December 1812
Sister Abigal Foster [wife of Joel] died at 2 o'clock in the morning

He never diagnosed the disease that had slipped inside the cabin. He offered no cure. The old remedies recorded in his diary must not have applied. After recording the death of his sister-in-law, Ichabod wrote only "snow." I feel his energy draining, like a well running dry. His entries are short. Was he overcome with sadness? Sickness? Both? Did he know he had no cure for what was overcoming his cabin-bound family? The next deaths are entered in someone else's handwriting.

24 December 1812
Joel Foster died

27 December 1812
Sam'll died in the night

I envision the one-room log home crowded with crying children and frightened parents, a bewildered grandmother my age. One window. One door. Engulfed with snow. Ichabod's diary says that three feet blanketed the log walls when New Year's Day 1813 dawned. He might have been unconscious by then. He died some time that day.

1 January 1813
Ichabod Foster died in the 74 year of his age

Had they died right here? Are their graves somewhere near? My bottom is chilled from sitting on the log. Melting snow settles in my lap. A distant crow cries out, breaking the silence. I can't make myself get up. I picture Benjamin holding his father's body. Was it wrapped in a blanket? Was it buried in the snow? Did a wolf dig it up? By then, three bodies were hidden somewhere outside the cabin.

I look at my watch. Forty minutes have passed since I walked up the logging road, daydreaming, imagining faces of somber people passing through my reflective lenses. Margaret would be wondering if I slid into a ditch.

My boots squish in the soggy snow. Am I stepping over the remains of Ichabod's potato patch? I feel empty, like a bird's nest in winter. I found Lot 51, but it's too large to comprehend, subdivided numerous times. I don't see anything that resembles a grave, that final border piece in Ichabod's life, or the remains of the log cabin where he died.

Maybe I wasn't meant to find them—this time. Is something lurking, buried behind my thoughts, like dead leaves waiting to be turned over? I feel as if he is breathing on my neck, his soul slipping through the snowflakes. Why? Maybe it's the wind or my wanting not to let go. What is he asking me to do? Search deeper into his written words? I pick up a sliver of bark, a tangled vine, a palm full of mud, and seal them in a plastic bag. I can't return to Lopez Island without something from Lot 51. I walk down the hill surrounded in a veil of sadness, sprinkled with feelings of pride in our common roots.

❦

"I was ready to send the posse after you," Margaret says as I stomp my boots on her office doormat. "Any luck?"

"No." How could I tell her that I was sure he was there with me, and that that was what really mattered. Our journey together was a success. We both made it, in our own way and our own time.

"I'm not surprised you didn't find a grave," she says. "Here, let me show you something I worked on while you were gone.

Death grips the Foster cabin on Lot 51 December 1812 and January 1813

Jan.ʳ 31 Days 1813

January 1 1813
Ichabod Foster Died
in his 72 [...] of his age

Abigal Foster Died
December the 21 1819
in the thirty seventh
year of her age

the wife of Ichabod Foster
Susannah Foster X
Died February the 24
1720 in the twenty
fifth year of her
age

I know he stayed in the restored Stone cabin down the road. Did you notice it when you drove in? A family lives there now, so I don't know if you can visit it."

"I'll photograph it from the street when I leave," I say.

Margaret opens a file labeled Foster. She has made copies of Ichabod's diary pages describing this common man whose life was wedged between two wars with Great Britain, who continued venturing to wild, unsettled lands until he was an old man. His colorful puzzle contains stories of family, friends, and farming, cures for colds, election results and religious squabbles, wrapped around snowstorms, droughts, and the arrival of the first robin each spring. Seeing Margaret's file with Ichabod's name reminds me of all the other spots along his trail that now have his writings filed away.

"Margaret, I imagine Ichabod's diary resting on his writing table in that log cabin on Lot 51, his quill pen across the page marked January 1813," I say. "Who picked it up? Crushed by disease and death, who thought to save the diary? If only those pages could speak?"

"You keep looking," Margaret says. "The answers will come."

Research is my passion, not the struggle to formulate words so that others will connect to Ichabod. When my spirit doesn't rise up to meet my dreams, when I'm ready to quit because I've bumped into another brick wall, I feel a nudge. Ichabod didn't quit when this wagon wheels were mired in mud or stuck in a snowbank. He kept on walking from Whiting to Willink. What kind of person would do this? Why was I, after two hundred years, the ancestor driven to resurrect Ichabod? I believe the answers will surface someday.

How can I honor the life of this ordinary person who had no merits to mark the pages of history books? Aren't the common ones worth remembering? Without men such as Ichabod, whose fingers dropped the first corn kernels in virgin soil, whose arms swung axes against old-growth trunks, the frontier would have remained wild.

"Margaret, could I create my own puzzle piece to complete the borders of Ichabod's life?" I ask. "Could I have a grave marker made and place it in the oldest cemetery in town?"

"Why not?" she says, a mischievous twinkle in her eye. "Ichabod could go directly down a bit from Erasmus Briggs. Actually, he could rest next to the Spooner monument we found floating around down the Cattaraugus Creek without a body. The stone was brought up and placed in Fairview Cemetery. I think the two would go nicely together."

"Sounds like a plan. I'll see you next year, Margaret."

Chapter Seven

ICHABOD'S BURIAL

The scent of freshly mowed grass seeps into my nostrils. Damp blades stick to my shoes as I walk alone, reading inscriptions, watching the September sunlight ripple across the graves in the pioneer section of Fairview Cemetery. I spot Erasmus Briggs's stone, ornate and fitting for the famous citizen who wrote *History of the Original Town of Concord* in 1883. Nearby, I see the Spooner monument, the one Margaret said was found floating down Cattaraugus Creek with no bodies. The inscriptions speak of winter storms aging their names, creating grooves for moss to grow. Graves arouse a visceral sense of longing in me. I yearn to hear their inhabitants' stories, to step through their cabin doors, to know how they coped with death, to see them celebrating an abundant harvest.

I notice an old-style granite stone, smooth, simple, erect, resting in recently tilled dirt next to the Spooner family. It looks old. It feels new. I stop to read the inscription.

In Memory of

Ichabod Foster
Born 10 April 1740
Attleborough, MA

Died 1 January 1813
Married 5 June 1768
Susannah Carr Foster
Exeter, RI
Died 24 February 1820
Concord, NY

Ichabod has a grave. Gratitude fills my soul as I run my
fingers across the stone. Margaret had kept her word about
Ichabod's neighbors in the old cemetery. She had lured me
back to Concord to participate in a celebration of his life and
a dedication of his stone. A local funeral director arranged
for the marker, carved in a simple, common motif. I will lay
Ichabod to rest with words, without his bones, where his spirit
will embrace his natural elements—blizzards, thunderstorms,
and sunshine.

Is my Uncle Warren smiling? Is he recalling the Thanksgiving Day thirty years ago when he handed me the family notes
and sent me on my search? Ichabod's diary filled in the blanks
and documented the day he died.

I see death as a stone dropped in a pond. When it first
shatters the surface, it casts a sharp sting, like the one I felt
on the day my brother died and my father soon followed. As
death ages, it softens, making room for new life. The ripples
on the surface grow wider; more ancestors appear. They blend
with my family in graves across the Midwest and Northeast, a
line eleven generations long. Did Ichabod want me to find his
place in my lineage, to follow his trail?

" . . . some [people] point to ancestors who have beckoned
to them, led them, or otherwise made their presence known.
It appears that untold numbers of ancestors have asked to be
understood and to have their stories told fully and accurately,"
wrote Helen Hinchliff in *Psychic Roots*.[1]

I see parents walking across the grass, carrying folding chairs. Their children, dressed in period costumes, spread blankets on the ground near his grave. The celebration of Ichabod's life had been front-page news for two weeks. A copy of a diary page illustrated one article, with a cutline reading, "Pack up the kids and the lawn chairs and plan on attending this rare occasion in our town."[2]

Margaret is putting out a plate of oatmeal cookies on the dessert table under an oak tree. She notices me standing by the stone and walks over.

"How do you like it?" she asks. "I told you he'd have good neighbors. Here's a copy of the program. I think you'll like it, too."

"You certainly deliver on your word," I say. "I hope Ichabod likes what we're doing. At least his isn't the only stone without bones. Do you think we're crazy putting a marker in a cemetery that didn't exist when he died?"

"I don't care," Margaret says. "We're having fun and feeling a bit of our old history at the same time. He's around here somewhere."

I read the program. The president of the cemetery association will welcome everyone. A young mother who is raising her children on a part of Lot 51 will sing *Amazing Grace*. Her husband will read the benediction. Children will recite passages from Ichabod's diary. A cobbler's bench and tools, honoring one of Ichabod's trades, are assembled near the podium. A local fiddle group will play period pieces while children place potted plants around the stone.

"Margaret, you'd make a good politician," I say. "You haven't left anyone out on this program."

"Here's a list of the flowers," Margaret says. "They were ones from his time—coreopsis, feverfew, Rudbeckia, shasta daisies, and Johnny-jump-ups."

"Do you know what passages the children will read?" I ask.

"No," says Margaret. "I gave copies of the diary pages to the fourth-grade teacher at the Springville–Griffith Institute School. The children picked what they wanted to read. His diary has certainly sparked their interest in their community and its early history."

"We should begin," Margaret says. "Can you believe it? I think around one hundred and fifty people are gathered here in the cemetery."

As my place on the program arrives, I pick up the notes I had left beside Ichabod's grave. I look at the children in the front row, and begin to speak.

"Try to imagine a bitter-cold, snowy day in late November. The area surrounding us here is dense, dark, covered with old-growth trees. There is no community, no church or school. Families live many miles apart. You live in a crowded one-room log cabin. Wolves and bears roam the Indian trails running across your land. There are no roads. You notice oxen pulling a wagon."

The children's eyes stare at mine.

"There is a young girl sitting on her mother's lap, bundled under a quilt, shivering as the wind off Lake Erie blows her bonnet," I say. "Two men trudge alongside the wagon, heads down, their boots worn through their soles after walking nearly six hundred miles from Whiting, Vermont.

"We all have a story to tell," I say. "This is Ichabod's, as I imagine him arriving here in 1811."

I describe my great-great-great-grandfather, a farmer who made shoes and boots for his family and friends, and wove the first basket in Willink. He recorded the return of the first robin each spring, and the days he planted corn and cucumbers. Ichabod's writings reveal an intelligent, observant, disciplined man who recorded facts. He ignored feelings. He was a risk taker in the wilderness who scrutinized his natural surroundings.

I glance across the crowd. All are watching me, listening. I'm happy that Ichabod will rest here. I close by telling these citizens of this rural community in western New York that I believe Ichabod would want us to value our written words, the ones recorded when our pencils scroll across pieces of paper. If he had lived in our Internet-driven society, where computers send e-mails flying back and forth with poor punctuation and grammar, he would have worn out his delete button.

"I believe as long as someone remembers us we are not dead," I say. "We live through them, as I believe Ichabod lives through us today. His handwritten words have made this happen."

Ichabod's remembrance ends with the benediction. People start to mingle around the refreshment table, sipping lemonade, sharing tales of their early lives in Concord, asking if I'm going to continue to search Lot 51 for his bones. Soon families are opening car doors, packing children into back seats and chairs into trunks. Dave, the town historian, taps me on the shoulder.

"You want to go poking around for those bones again? The ground is dry. I know where his log cabin once stood."

"Do you really?" I ask. "I wish I had met you when I was here before."

We help Margaret and her volunteers pack up her table and chairs. Dave loads the cobbler's bench and tools into his pickup truck.

"Margaret, Dave and I are going on a bone search," I say. "Want to join us?"

"I'll come along," she says. "But I'll stay in the car."

We park about a mile from the cemetery in the driveway of an empty white clapboard house on the Boston–Springville Road.

"This was the Amos Stanbro place," Dave says. "He was the first person to take title to this part of Lot 51 in 1834. Based on Briggs's description and your diary, this is where the Foster cabin stood. Want to climb up the hill out back and look for the apple orchard—and maybe a grave?"

"Not me," says Margaret. "I'll wait here."

"Let's go," I say.

I change into my hiking boots. We climb the small hill as sunlight weaves around the thick maple trunks. Tangled grapevines hang from ancient oaks. My boots rustle the leaves. I photograph Dave in front of a massive oak that he says probably was a sapling when Ichabod planted his grapevines here. He and I wander in different directions, looking for clues of life, of death.

"Please, Ichabod, help me find you," I whisper. "Guide me to your real grave."

Leaves cling to a towering cherry tree, probably planted after his family left for Niagara County. I see Dave approaching.

"This was definitely an orchard," he says.

"Find any evidence of a grave?" I ask.

"Not yet, but I'm going to keep trying."

I start from one point on the ground and walk around in expanding circles. I don't know why. I see nothing but leaves, fallen logs, and low brush. What do I expect to see? A gravestone? A wooden marker would have decayed. On my next circle, I notice a mound of rocks. I hadn't seen them before. Several yards away, I notice another low mound, smooth and spread out.

"Dave, can you tell me why these rocks would be piled here? This land was never cleared for plowing."

He walks toward me and kneels down beside the first mound.

"Could be," he says, taking out a tape measure. "Six feet by about three feet. That's a good grave size for the old days."

I'm afraid to believe what I want to believe. Why am I not satisfied with the dedication of a new stone in the pioneer cemetery? Is that fabrication? Is this real?

"They would have piled the graves with rocks to keep the wolves from eating the bodies," Dave says. "The mounds have worn down after nearly two hundred years. With four bodies to bury at one time, they probably put two in each grave."

"Couldn't these be Stanbro graves?" I ask.

"No. Their family is in the old cemetery," Dave says.

A rush of adrenaline races through my veins. A whiff of air tickles my nose. Is intuition a truth deeper than fact?

"I know he's here," I say. "I feel it. He has to be."

I look at Dave.

"Do you have a shovel in your truck?" I ask.

"No, and if I did, you couldn't start digging," he says. "The law is sticky about exhuming a body without a court order. Besides, we are trespassing on private property."

A body. I only want a bone to compare our DNA. Private property? No one lives here.

I sit on the leaves beside the first grave. Who else but me cares if Ichabod's bones are beneath me? Suddenly, I feel as ridiculous as I did driving the back roads across New York State, asking myself what I was learning. Is this search more about me than Ichabod? My husband and I bought fifteen acres of third-growth Douglas fir twenty years ago, graded a dirt driveway, dug a well, and built a log cabin. In Whiting, as in Willink, I discovered living with nature is as ingrained in me as the texture of my brown hair and the shade of my blue eyes. Searching for what lives in me that lived in Ichabod, I see reflected what pulled me to a rural farming island in the Pacific Northwest. For generations my family traveled on the fringe, challenged by opportunities and adventures in unsettled places. Our gene pool flows in circles, expands, remains the same.

"Why would you want to dig for bones? Dave says. "You won't know if they belong to Ichabod or his son or his brother."

"Maybe there's a way," I say, struggling to deny the question. "I'm going back to tell Margaret what we found."

"I'll measure the second mound and be right down," Dave says.

"Margaret, we found two piles of stones that could be graves," I say. "Maybe I'm overanxious, but they feel right."

"Well, what are you going to do now, move his bones or his cemetery stone?" she asks.

"Neither. Dave says it's illegal to start digging. You can't do it without court approval."

"Darn. Maybe I can think of another way," Margaret says.

Dave joins us in the driveway. "I think we found the Fosters," he says. "The second mound is identical to the first.

"I'll bring a professional to assess the site," he adds.

"Please e-mail me with the results," I say as the sun is sliding behind the far hill on Lot 51.

"I'll phone if I find a bootleg gravedigger," Margaret says. "We can pretend we are planting wildflowers and dig a little deeper than necessary."

I hug Margaret. "Thank you for keeping Ichabod alive in old Willink," I say. "Do you think you can find a digger with a bit of curiosity?"

"You know me," Margaret says with a twinkle.

Epilogue

THE MIGRATION OF THE DIARY

Fluorescent light flickered across the table, reminding me of the room in Rhode Island where I first touched Ichabod's Vermont indenture of 1761. The curator slid a document in front of me. He placed a pen beside it. Ichabod's diary, crumbling around the edges, rested next to me in the windowless room. No one spoke. I began reading the contract to myself.

I, Julie F. Van Camp . . . do hereby make a free gift of the material specified below to the New England Historic Genealogical Society and its successor organizations.

Being the sole owner of the material, I give this material, and any additions which I may make to it, unencumbered to the New England Historic Genealogical Society and do declare that I made the gift of my own free will and without influence. . . .

The line for the donor's signature came first. Below it, a witness would sign, and then the curator. I picked up the pen. Cherry Fletcher Bamberg, who helped me decipher Ichabod's cures and Old English script, signed on the witness line. Timothy Salls accepted Ichabod on behalf of the Society.

Why was I parting with this treasure that had traveled with my ancestors across the country, surviving through eight generations, tucked in trunks and dresser drawers? Why didn't I keep it in my safe deposit box on Lopez Island?

I felt as though I were putting a child up for adoption, dropping him off in a home that was best for his future. I could visit at any time. This contract was Ichabod's life insurance policy, one in which the Society promised to protect his writings forever. He would live through his sketches and his script. His doodlings and daily weather reports would be cataloged for Internet viewing. Would Ichabod feel embarrassed at his public exposure?

I sat back in my chair, trying to picture life in Ichabod's log cabin during that winter of 1812. Did the same disease that had killed his son, his brother, and his sister-in-law a few days before he took his last breath kill him as well? Ichabod had intended to continue recording his daily events, his handwriting still strong and steady at age seventy-two. Atop the next page, his heading was the usual—month, number of days, and year—January 31 Days 1813. Down the left side, he had written the numbers 1 through 31. Next to that column, the first number was 6, telling me he that he had died on the sixth day of the week, Saturday.

Who picked up his diary amidst the disease and death eating away at the Foster family huddled in the small cabin engulfed by snow, grieving over four deaths in eleven days? Somewhere, somehow, Albro, my great-great-grandfather, acquired his father's diary. I don't know how many thousands of miles it had traveled before it rested finally on this table in the A. Stanton Avery Special Collections section in Boston on October 9, 2003.

"Thank you both for witnessing and endorsing my decision. I know the diary will be safe from further decay," I said. "Can you leave it on the table a little longer? My son, Tom, and his eleven-year-old daughter, Rachel, should step off the elevator at any moment. They have never seen the diary."

"Certainly, but don't handle it without putting on cotton gloves," Timothy said. "You'll find some in that box on the card catalog. Do you think we'll ever receive the original of the second diary, the one from 1809 to 1813 that you copied for us?"

"I hope so," I said. "A fifth cousin keeps it in a box in his dresser drawer in Beverly, Kansas. I'm grateful he was willing to make a copy."

Soon, three generations of Ichabod's descendants sat alone in the research room reading the diary. I felt as though we were participating in a wake before the burial. We'd slipped on gloves. I'd picked up my magnifying glass and begun reading accounts of Ichabod harvesting wheat, bartering corn for nails, disagreeing with his Baptist brethren, making shoes for his children.

"Oh, Gammie, look at the sailing ships he drew," Rachel said. "Look at those tiny birds flying across the page. He was an artist. I could paint pictures of his life," she said. "What did he look like?"

"I wish I could tell you, but he died before photography was developed," I said. "The oldest family photo I have is one of his grandson, Azariah, your great-great-great-grandfather. In that black-and-white photo, he had a bushy beard, a balding head, and a slim, short frame. I imagine his eyes were blue, like yours, your dad's, and mine. You can complete the picture in your imagination."

"That will be fun," Rachel said. "Where did he live?"

"In the wilderness when wolves raced in packs in western Vermont before the Revolutionary War broke out," I said. "He died near the shores of Lake Erie in New York when the British were firing cannons over Buffalo during the War of 1812."

Ichabod sketches a boat   September 1790

Tom picked up the diary. "The drawings and writing are so small. Look at this line: 'The red cow went to bull.' This man had a way with words."

"What happened to the diary when Ichabod died?" Rachel asked.

"I believe several generations of Foster women protected it, wrapping it in their muslin dresses or quilts as they climbed into their wagons heading west to Ohio and Kansas in the 1800s."

Rachel and Tom continued to page through the diary. I leaned back in my chair and thought about the diary's long migration. I believe Ichabod's wife kept it after he died, but I don't know if she remained with her oldest son. If Benjamin had it, why didn't he record the death of his wife, Lydia Beach, in 1816 and his two-year-old daughter in 1818? He didn't leave Lot 51 until 1820. On the last page, January 1813, outlined by Ichabod, someone recorded his death on January 1, 1813, "in the 72 year of his age"; the death of his wife, Susannah, on February 14, 1820, "in the seventy-fifth year of her life"; and the death of their daughter, Abigail, on December 21, 1814, "in the thirty-seventh year of her life." The remainder of the diary is blank. Who lifted it from Susannah's trunk?

Could her youngest son, Albro, have taken it? His wife, Rispa Doane Foster, appears in the 1820 census as head of household in Bakersfield, Vermont, an isolated outpost, nestled below Cold Hollow Mountain near the Canadian border. Had Albro returned to western New York to mourn his mother's death? Did he pack the diary in his saddlebags when he left the Holland Purchase lands to return home? Was he trotting along the Genesee Trail on the day that the census taker knocked on his door in Bakersfield? I can only piece together the possibilities based on the movement of the family recorded in land deeds and census documents.

Albro and Rispa spent their married life traveling with the Doane family from Jefferson County, New York, back to Bakersfield, Vermont, and returning to Jefferson County, where their youngest child, Ann Jeannette, was born on October 9, 1831. When she was eighteen months old, the family, along with several of Rispa's brothers, moved to Medina County, Ohio. Was the diary packed in a trunk as they traveled? The notes my Uncle Warren gave me thirty years ago on Thanksgiving Day read:

Albro Foster. Lived at Bakersfield VT and Sackets Harbor N.Y. served during the War of 1812, was in battles of Sackets Harbor, Ellisburg and Little York. Moved to Medina Co O about 1834 and in 1857 moved to Lorain Co O near Elyria where he died May 15, 1874. Buried Ridgeville, O. Rispa Doane Foster. Died and buried same place as above—July 24, 1879.

After her parents died, Ann Jeannette and her husband, Richard Hinckley, and their four children moved west. She carried the diary from Lorain County, Ohio, to Lincoln County, Kansas, in a covered wagon in 1880 and protected it from prairie fires and dust storms until she died there in 1927. Three more generations of women treasured the diary until I received it in 1997 and brought it to Lopez Island.

"I'd love to sit down and read this through someday," Tom said.

"Me, too," said Rachel.

Ichabod's great-great-great-great-great-granddaughter had touched his fingerprints. I sensed she wouldn't let Ichabod slip from her memory.

"It's five o'clock," Timothy said. "We're closing now. You can come back any time tomorrow."

He slid the diary into a brown envelope. As we waited for the elevator to reach the fifth floor, I was imagining Rachel's grandchildren fifty years from now peering at the pages of tiny Old English script. What questions would these descendants of Ichabod ask? "What is an earmark?" "What is quinsy?"

31 July 1794
A cure for quinsy take a white wesel skin and ware it
on the throat which will prevent it come

12 August 1794
Our earmark a half crop the underside of the right ear

August 1811
There has been seen a blazing star in the Northwest sence abut
the first of September

10 September 1811
Rachel Beach set out with her family for the Holland Purches

If ancestors are remembered, I believe they never die. They live in our souls, in our imaginations, in our hearts, in our writing. Had I been searching for Ichabod or had he been searching for me? Each spring on Lopez Island, I listen for the return of his first robin.

The man who feels no sentiment of veneration for the memory of his forefathers, who has no natural regard for his ancestors, or his kindred, is himself unworthy of kindred or remembrance.

—Daniel Webster

ENDNOTES

Prologue

1. H. P. Smith, ed., *History of Addison County Vermont: With Illustrations and Biographical Sketches of Some of Its Prominent Men and Pioneers* (Syracuse, NY: D. Mason & Company, 1886), 726; Harold and Elizabeth Webster, *Our Whiting: Story of a Small Vermont Town* (Rutland: Academy Books, 1976), 19.
2. Cynthia Meyerson, e-mail, July 23, 1997.
3. Ibid., e-mail, July 24, 1997.
4. Ichabod Foster, *Diary 1785–1813* (Boston: New England Historic Genealogical Society, R. Stanton Avery Special Collections Department, unpublished original through 1808, copy of original 1809-1813 (original owned by Richard Cole, Lincoln County, Kansas), 282 pages. Mss #716.
5. Marjorie Goad, e-mail, January 12, 2001.

Chapter One

1. Rich Stattler, processed by, *John Henry Lydius Papers* (Providence: Rhode Island Historical Society, Manuscripts Department, 2000, Mss #545), 1.
2. Matt Bushell Jones, *Vermont in the Making 1750–1779* (Hamden, CT: Archon Books, 1968), 145.

3. Stattler, *John Henry Lydius Papers*, 1.
4. John Daggett, *Sketch of the History of Attleborough from Its Settlement to the Present Time* (Dedham, MA: H. Mann Printer 1834), 44.
5. http://www.u-s-history.com.
6. http://en.wikipedia.org/wiki/James_Otis.
7. John Foster, letter to James Otis (Boston: Massachusetts Historical Society library, March 10, 1748/9).
8. J. Kevin Graffagnino, *The Shaping of Vermont: From Wilderness to the Centennial 1749–1877* (Rutland: Vermont Heritage Press; Bennington: Bennington Museum, 1983), 3.
9. Jones, *Vermont in the Making*, 143.
10. Stattler, *John Henry Lydius Papers*, 1.
11. Abby Maria Hemenway, ed. *Vermont Historical Gazetteer,* vol. 3 (Claremont, NH: The Claremont Manufacturing Co., 1877), 554.
12. Rutland Vermont Land Deeds, vol. 1 (Vermont: Rutland), 139.
13. Cherry Fletcher Bamberg, "John Rice, Jr. of Warwick, Rhode Island," *Rhode Island Roots*, vol. 27, no. 1 (Providence: March 2001), 4.
14. David E. Potter, *Early Land Grants & Title Controversy Clarendon Vermont 1761–1976* (Rutland, VT: Academy Books, 2nd printing, 1982), 10.
15. Harral Ayres, *Great Trails and the Associated Paths of the Pioneers* (Boston: Meador Publishing Co., 1940), 55, 66, 297.
16. James Truslow Adams, editor in chief, *The Atlas of American History* (New York: Charles Scribner's Sons, 1943), 7.
17. Jan Albers, *Hands on the Land: A History of the Vermont Landscape* (Cambridge, MA: MIT Press, 2000), 82.
18. Walter Hill Crockett, *Vermont: The Green Mountain State*, vol. 1 (Burlington: Vermont Farm Bureau, 1938), 258.

19. Lewis D. Stillwell, *Migration from Vermont (1776–1860)* (Montpelier: Vermont Historical Society, 1948), 65.

20. Ibid., 80.

21. www.u-s-history.com/pages/h645.html.

22. Albers, *Hands on the Land,* 79.

23. Ibid., 88.

24. Crockett, *Vermont: The Green Mountain State,* 261.

25. Mary Green Nye, ed., *State Papers of Vermont, vol. VII, New York Land Patents 1688–1786 covering land now included in the state of Vermont (not including Military Patents)* (Montpelier: Secretary of State, 1947), 286.

26. Ibid., 287.

27. Stillwell, *Migration from Vermont,* 87.

28. David M. Ludlum, *Social Ferment in Vermont: 1791–1850* (New York: AMS Press, Inc., 1966), 20.

29. Ibid., 21.

30. Nathan Perkins, *A Narrative of a Tour Through the State of Vermont from April 27 to June 12, 1789 by the Rev'd Nathan Perkins of Hartford* (Woodstock, VT: The Yankee Bookshop, 1937), 116.

Chapter Two

1. Henry Steele Commager and Richard B. Morris, eds., *The Spirit of "Seventy-Six": The Story of the American Revolution as Told by Participants* (New York: Harper & Row, 1967), 568.

2. A. M. Caverly, *History of the Town of Pittsford, Vermont with Biographical Sketches and Family Records* (Rutland: Charles E. Tuttle Co., 1872), 122.

3. Ibid., 117.

4. James E. Petersen, *Otter Creek: The Indian Road* (Salisbury, VT: Dunmore House, 1990), 56.

5. Gordon S. Wood, reviewer, *Iron Tears: America's Battle for Freedom, Britain's Quagmire: 1775–1783* by Stanley Weintraub (*New York Review of Books*, vol. 52, no. 7, April 18, 2005), 33.

6. Ibid.

7. Petersen, *Otter Creek*, 59.

8. Ibid., 80.

9. Benjamin Foster, in *Abstracts of Revolutionary War Pension Files*, p. 549 #S9312, application 25, September 1833, Essex County, New York, age 71, resident of Moriah, NY; also *Abstract of Rev. War Pension Files,* S5421, Vt. Line (National Archives and Records Administration, General Reference Branch (NNRG-P), 7th and Pennsylvania Avenue, NW, Washington, DC 20408) p. 1239; John E. Goodrich, comp., *State of Vermont Rolls of the Soldiers in the Revolutionary War 1775–1783* (Rutland: Charles E. Tuttle Co., 1904), 140, 477.

10. Lewis D. Stillwell, *Migration from Vermont (1776–1860)* (Montpelier: Vermont Historical Society, 1948), 65.

11. E. B. De Fonblanque, derived from *Life and Correspondence of Right Hon. John Burgoyne: Political and Military Episodes in the Latter Half of the Eighteenth Century, 1876,* pp. 317–318: http://www.nndo/com/people/238/000050088/May 20, 2006.

12. Mary Green Nye, ed., *State Papers of Vermont, vol. VII, New York Land Patents 1688–1786 covering land now included in the state of Vermont (not including Military Patents)* (Montpelier: Secretary of State, 1947), 286–87.

13. Ibid., *State Papers of Vermont, vol. VI, Sequestration, Confiscation and Sales of Estates* (Montpelier: Secretary of State, 1941), 79–81.

14. Ibid., 80.

15. Ibid.

16. David E. Potter, "Early Land Grants & Title Controversy" *Clarendon, VT 1761–1976* (Rutland: Academy Books, 2nd printing, 1982), 12.
17. Ibid.
18. Donn Devine, "Clues in Old Cemeteries," *Ancestry*, vol. 22, no. 1 (January–February 2004), 52.
19. Ibid.
20. *Middlebury (VT) Mercury*, January 28, 1803, 1.
21. Harold and Elizabeth Webster, *Our Whiting: Story of a Small Vermont Town* (Rutland: Academy Books, 1976), 19.

Chapter Three

1. Henry Z Jones Jr., *More Psychic Roots: Further Adventures in Serendipity & Intuition in Genealogy* (Baltimore: Genealogical Publishing Co., 1997), 222. E-mail from Henry Z Jones Jr., May 25, 2006: "I'm up to about 1,300 stories/experiences now shared by our genealogical colleagues from around the world: FUN."
2. Louis B. Wright, *Everyday Life in Colonial America* (New York: Putnam, 1966), 236.
3. Jan Albers, *Hands on the Land: A History of the Vermont Landscape* (Cambridge, MA: MIT Press, 2000), 105.
4. Cathy Hartt, e-mail, May 25, 2006.
5. Laurel Thatcher Ulrich, *A Midwife's Tale: The Life of Martha Ballard Based on Her Diary 1785–1812* (New York: Vintage Books, 1991).
6. Ibid., 12.
7. Ibid., 183.
8. Ibid., 155, 156, 157.
9. Ibid., 188.

10. Adelaide Hechtlinger, *The Seasonal Hearth: The Woman at Home in Early America* (Woodstock, NY: Overlook Press, 1977), 93.

11. Timothy Salls, manuscripts curator, New England Historic Genealogical Society. Personal interview, Boston, October 9, 2003.

12. *How to Read a 200-Year-Old-Document*,earlyamerica .com/howto.html, May 20, 2006.

13. John Daggett, *Sketch of the History of Attleborough from Its Settlement to the Present Time* (Dedham, MA: H. Mann Printer, 1834), 90.

14. Julie Foster Van Camp, "Ichabod's Diary: A Window to His World," *Ancestry*, vol. 18, no 2 (March–April 2000), 61.

15. Jones, *More Psychic Roots*, 222.

16. www.thanksgiving.org/2us.html, accessed August 21, 2005.

17. Bernard Swartz, *American Christmas Origins,* www.bsu.edu/ web/ 01bkswartz/ xmaspub.html, accessed May 24, 2006.

18. Albers, *Hands on the Land*, 108.

19. Ted Collier, *Natural Compass: Windfall Orchard: Vermont Apples in the Champlain Valley, 1997*.www.naturecompass. org/orchard/remembering.html, accessed May 24, 2006.

20. http://en.wikipedia.org/wiki/Potash, accessed May 24, 2006.

21. Susan Peden, education coordinator, Henry Sheldon Museum. Personal interview, Middlebury, VT, October 13, 2003; e-mail, October 31, 2003.

22. Hechtlinger, *The Seasonal Hearth*, 97.

23. Harold and Elizabeth Webster, *Our Whiting: Story of a Small Vermont Town.* (Rutland: Academy Books, 1976), 23.

24. Leonard Everett Fisher, *The Shoemakers* (New York: Benchmark Books, 1998), 34.
25. Ibid.
26. Lewis D. Stillwell, *Migration from Vermont (1776–1860)* (Montpelier: Vermont Historical Society, 1948), 112.
27. Whiting, Vermont, Land Deeds, Book 3, 38.

Chapter Four

1. Lewis D. Stillwell, *Migration from Vermont (1776–1860)* (Montpelier: Vermont Historical Society, 1948), 112.
2. *Orwell Baptist Church Minutes 1787–1805*, December 24, 1787 (Orwell, VT: Town Clerk's Office, Connie Hotits, clerk, 1992).
3. Stillwell, *Migration from Vermont*, 112.
4. *Orwell Baptist Church Minutes 1787–1805*, May 30, 1791.
5. Ibid., June 3, 1791.
6. Ibid., September 6, 1800.
7. Ibid., April 25, 1801.
8. Ibid., August 6, 1800.
9. David Hackett Fischer, *Albion's Seed: Four British Folkways in America* (New York: Oxford University Press, 1989), 16.
10. Hon. Barnes Frisbie, *The History of Middletown, Vermont in Three Discourses* (Poultney: Middletown Springs Historical Society, 1975), 81.
11. Ibid., 82.
12. Ibid.
13. Ibid., 87.

Chapter Five

1. Alden Beaman, comp., *Rhode Island Vital Records, New Series, Vol. 4, Washington County RI Births from Probate Records* (Princeton, MA: 1978), 59.

2. Arthur A. Carr, *The Carr Book: Sketches of the lives of many of the descendants of Robert and Caleb Carr, whose arrival on this continent in 1635 began the American story of our family* (Ticonderoga, NY: Arthur A. Carr, 1945; Rutland: Tuttle Publishing Co.); Edson I. Carr, *Carr Family Records* (Rockton, IL: Herald Printing House, 1894).

3. Dorothy Higson White, comp., *Descendants of Roger Williams, Book III: The Sayles Line Through His Daughter Mary Williams* (publication sponsored by Roger Williams Family Association, gift to the Rhode Island Historical Society Library, November 7, 2002), 8–13.

4. Cherry Fletcher Bamberg, trans., *The Diary of Capt. Samuel Tillinghast of Warwick, Rhode Island 1757–1766* (Special Publication no. 3, Rhode Island Genealogical Society, Providence, 2000): 246–47. At bottom of page 246, Benjamin Carr made his will July 6, 1762, and it was proved at Exeter September 14, 1762 (Exeter Town Council and Probate Records, 3: 173–74.) He left his widow, Mary, with a very large, very young family: five sons under twenty-one and five daughters under eighteen. *The Search for "Uncle Carr"* by Cherry Fletcher Bamberg, unpublished summary of evidence that surmises this Carr connection, October 2003.

5. *History of Washington Co., New York 1737–1878* (Interlaken, NY: Heart of the Lakes Publishing, 1991), 375.

6. http://www.saratoga.org/battle1777/history.html, accessed October 30, 2003.

7. Kenneth B. Shaw, *Broadalbin Then and Now: A Pictorial History* (Broadalbin, NY: K.B.S., 1973), 5–6.

8. Edwin M. Knights Jr., "In Pursuit of Your Medical Pedigree," *Family Chronicles* (September–October 1999): 47.

9. Beverly Downing, "Pounds of Cure," *Family Chronicle* (January–February 1999): 45.

10. David Curtis Dearborn, "Ancestors on the Move: Migrations Out of New England," *New England Ancestors,* vol. 3, no. 2 (Spring 2002): 13.

11. Samuel Day, *Record 572,866 LDS Samuel Day, Attleboro, 1761, Last Will and Testament, 11 Mar 1761* (Salt Lake City: Probate Records of Bristol Co MA 1690–1881), #572,866; letter March 15, 2002, from Alice Bower, professional genealogist, Logan, UT.

12. Dearborn, "Ancestors on the Move," 11.

13. John Conlin, ed., *Western New York Heritage Press,* e-mail, January 31, 2005.

14. Lewis D. Stillwell, *Migration from Vermont (1776–1860)* (Montpelier: Vermont Historical Society, 1948), 135.

15. Ibid., 126.

16. Ibid., 129.

17. Ibid., 139.

18. Mabel Furner Jenks, *Lima 1788–1964, Outline of the History of Lima Written for the 175th Anniversary Celebration* (Saugerties, NY: Hope Farm Press, 1964), 10.

19. http://www.asaransom.com/genrinfo.htm, accessed May 25, 2006.

20. http://www.hollandlandoffice.com Weissend, Patrick R. *The Life and Times of Joseph Ellicott,* accessed May 6, 2006.

Chapter Six

1. Karen E. Livsey, *Western New York Land Transactions, 1804–1824: Extracted from the Archives of the Holland Land Company* (Baltimore: Genealogical Publishing Co., 1991), viii.

2. *Holland Land Company Records 1801–1884: A Guide to the Microfilm Edition* (Westfield, NY: Patton Library, 1992), 12.

3. Holland Land Company records 496, 1,414,984 (State University of New York at Fredonia, Reed Library, unindexed).

4. Ibid.

5. Ethelyn Weller, *North Collins Remembers, A Comprehensive History North Collins and Vicinity, 1941* (Google search, Ethelyn Weller, *North Collins Remembers*, chap. 1, accessed August 2, 2007).

6. Erasmus Briggs, *History of the Original Town of Concord: Being the Present Towns of Concord, Collins and Sardinia Erie County, New York* (Rochester: Union and Advertiser Company's Print, 1883).

7. Ibid., 368.

8. Ibid.

9. Ibid., 100.

10. Ibid., 106.

11. Ibid., 109.

12. Ibid., 107.

13. Ibid.

14. www.u-s-history.com/pg/h504/html accessed May 25, 2006.

15. *Index of Awards on Claim of Soldiers of the War of 1812*, as audited and allowed by the Adjutant and Inspector Generals, Pursuant to Chapter 176 of the Laws of 1859, New

York State Archives (Albany: Weed, Parsons and Co., 1860), Claim Index #12662 1850, 1959, and Rolls 1371, 2502, 446, 447.

16. Ibid., Roll 1371.

17. Ibid., Roll 2502.

18. Weller, *North Collins Remembers*, chap. 7.

19. Briggs, *History*, 145.

20. Michael S. McGurty, "Congress Would Not Meet Without a Victory to Announce Them: The American Invasion of Canada in 1812" (unpublished paper, October 2003), 12.

21. Ibid., 17.

22. Ibid., 29.

23. Ibid.; *Index of Awards*, Albro Foster Claim Index #12662, $95 to replace clothing and equipment while serving under Capt. Jehiel Dimocks, New York Militia, Major Benjamin Forsythe's Cavalry, January 20, 1813, to April 30, 1813.

24. McGurty, "Congress Would Not Meet," 29.

25. Ibid., 36.

26. http://freenet.buffalo.edu/bah/h/flint/index.html, accessed May 22, 2006.

Chapter Seven

1. Henry Z Jones Jr., *Psychic Roots: Serendipity & Intuition in Genealogy* (Baltimore: Genealogical Publishing Co., 1993), ix.

2. Paul Chapman, "Early Concord Pioneer Honored Sept. 10," *Springville* [New York] *Journal*, vol. 139, no. 34, September 1, 2005, 1.

BIBLIOGRAPHY

Adams, James Truslow, editor in chief. *The Atlas of American History*. New York: Charles Scribner's Sons, 1943.

Albers, Jan. *Hands on the Land: A History of the Vermont Landscape*. Cambridge, MA: MIT Press, 2000.

Ayres, Harral. *Great Trails and the Associated Paths of the Pioneers*. Boston: Meador Publishing Co., 1940.

Bamberg, Cherry Fletcher, ed. *The Diary of Samuel Tillinghast of Warwick, Rhode Island 1757–1766*. Greenville: Rhode Island Genealogical Society, 2000.

————. *Elder John Gorton & the Six Principle Baptist Church of East Greenwich, Rhode Island*. Greenville: Rhode Island Genealogical Society, 2001.

————. "John Rice, Jr. of Warwick, Rhode Island." *Rhode Island Roots*, vol. 27, no. 1 (March 2001).

Beaman, Alden, comp. *Rhode Island Vital Records, New Series, Vol. 4, Washington County RI Births from Probate Records*. Princeton, MA: 1978.

Beaman, Lucille B. "Abstracts of Exeter Wills." *Rhode Island Genealogical Register*, vol. 6, no. 1 (July 1983).

Benton, Josiah Henry. *Warning Out in New England 1656–1817*. Boston: W. B. Clark Co., 1911.

Bishop, Doris S., comp. *History of the Town of Orwell, Vermont*. Published by the town of Orwell, 1963.

Bottum, Hon. Roswell. *History of the Town of Orwell, Vermont from 1763–1851*. Rutland: Tuttle & Co., 1881.

Briggs, Erasmus. *History of the Original Town of Concord: Being the Present Towns of Concord, Collins and Sardinia Erie County, New York.* Rochester: Union and Advertiser Company's Print, 1883.

Carr, Arthur A. *The Carr Book: Sketches of the lives of many of the descendants of Robert and Caleb Carr, whose arrival on this continent in 1635 began the American story of our family.* Ticonderoga, NY: Arthur A. Carr, 1945; Rutland: Tuttle Publishing Co., Inc.

Carr, Edson I. *Carr Family Records.* Rockton, IL: Herald Printing House, 1894.

Caverly, A. M. *History of the Town of Pittsford, Vermont with Biographical Sketches and Family Records.* Rutland: Charles E. Tuttle Co., 1872.

Chapman, Paul. "Early Concord Pioneer Honored Sept. 10." *Springville* [New York] *Journal,* vol. 139, no 34, September 1, 2005.

Clarendon, Rutland County, Vermont Town Records 1761–1938. Montpelier: Genealogical Society of Utah, 1952.

Clarendon Vermont 1761–1976. Rutland: Academy Books, 2nd printing, 1982.

Commager, Henry Steele, and Richard B. Morris, eds. *The Spirit of "Seventy-Six": The Story of the American Revolution as told by participants.* New York: Harper & Row, 1967.

Crocker, Rev. Henry. *History of the Baptists in Vermont.* Bellows Falls, VT: P. H. Gobie Press, 1913.

Crockett, Walter Hill. *Vermont: The Green Mountain State,* vols. 1–3. Burlington: Vermont Farm Bureau, 1938; New York: The Century History Company, 1921.

Cutter, William Richard, A. M. *Genealogical and Personal Memoirs Relating to the Families of Boston and Eastern*

Massachusetts, vol. 2. New York: Lewis Historical Publishing Co., 1908.

Daggett, John. *Sketch of the History of Attleborough from Its Settlement to the Present Time.* Dedham, MA: H. Mann Printer, 1834.

Day, Samuel. *Record 572,866 LDS Samuel Day, Attleboro, 1761, Last Will and Testament, 11 Mar 1761.* Salt Lake City: Probate Records Bristol County, MA 1690–1881.

Dearborn, David Curtis. "Ancestors on the Move: Migrations Out of New England," *New England Ancestors*, vol. 3, no. 2 (Spring 2002).

De Fonblanque, E. B. Derived from *Life and Correspondence of Right Hon. John Burgoyne: Political and Military Episodes in the Latter Half of the Eighteenth Century*, 1876, 317–318, http://www.nndo/com/people/238/000050088/ May 20, 2006.

Devine, Donn. "Clues in Old Cemeteries," *Ancestry*, vol. 22, no. 1 (January–February 2004).

Dodge, Bertha S. *Tales of Vermont Ways and People.* Shelburne: The New England Press, 1996.

———. *Vermont by Choice: The Earliest Years.* Shelburne: The New England Press, 1987.

Downing, Beverly. "Pounds of Cure," *Family Chronicle* (January–February 1999).

Earle, Alice Morse. *Customs and Fashions in Old New England.* Rutland: Charles E. Tuttle Co., 1973.

———. *Home Life in Colonial Days.* Williamstown, MA: Corner House Publishers, 1984.

Evans, Paul Demund. *The Holland Land Company.* New York: Buffalo Historical Society, 1924.

Fischer, David Hackett. *Albion's Seed: Four British Folkways in America.* New York: Oxford University Press, 1989.

Fisher, Major General Carleton Edward and Sue Gray Fisher. *Soldiers, Sailors, and Patriots of the Revolutionary War: Vermont.* Camden, ME: Picton Press, 1992.

Fisher, Leonard Everett. *The Shoemakers.* New York: Benchmark Books, 1998.

Flanders, Stephen A. *Atlas of American Migration.* New York: Facts on File, Inc., 1998.

Foster, Benjamin. *Abstracts of Revolutionary War Pension Files,* p. 549 #S9312, application 25 September 1833, Essex County, New York, age 71, resident of Moriah, NY; also *Abstract of Rev. War Pension Files,* S5421, Vt. Line., p. 1239. National Archives and Records Administration, General Reference Branch (NNRG-P) 7th and Pennsylvania Avenue, NW, Washington, DC 20408.

Foster, Ichabod. *Diary 1785–1813.* Boston: New England Historic Genealogical Society, R. Stanton Avery Special Collections Department, unpublished original through 1808, copy of original 1809-1813 (original owned by Richard Cole, Lincoln County, KS). Mss #716, 282 pp.

Foster, John. Letter to James Otis, March 10, 1748/9. Boston: Massachusetts Historical Society library.

Frisbie, Hon. Barnes. *The History of Middletown, Vermont in Three Discourses.* Poultney: Middletown Springs Historical Society, 1975.

Goodrich, John E., comp. *State of Vermont Rolls of the Soldiers in the Revolutionary War 1775–1783.* Rutland: The Tuttle Company, 1904.

Graffagnino, J. Kevin. *The Shaping of Vermont: From Wilderness to the Centennial 1749–1877.* Rutland: Vermont Heritage Press; Bennington: Bennington Museum, 1983.

Greenwood, Val. *The Research Guide to American Genealogy*, 2nd ed. Baltimore: Genealogical Publishing Co., 1990.

Hamilton, Edward P. *Fort Ticonderoga: Key to a Continent*. Boston: Little, Brown and Company, 1964.

Haswell, Anthony. *Haswell's Vermont Almanac for the Year of our Lord 1792*. Bennington, VT: Anthony Haswell, 1792.

Hechtlinger, Adelaide. *The Seasonal Hearth: The Woman at Home in Early America*. Woodstock, NY: Overlook Press, 1977.

Hemenway, Abby Maria, ed. *The Vermont Historical Gazetteer or Magazine*, vol. 3, *Orleans & Rutland*. Claremont, NH: The Claremont Manufacturing Company, 1877; Salem, MA: Higginson Book Co., 1994.

_____. *Vermont Historical Gazetteer*: Addison, Bennington Counties. Burlington: 1867; Salem, MA: Higginson Book Co., 1994.

Hickey, Donald R. *The War of 1812*. Champaign: University of Illinois Press, 1989.

A History of the Town of Orwell, Vermont: Past & Present. Orwell: Orwell Historical Society, 1988.

History of Washington Co., New York 1737–1878. Interlaken, NY: Heart of the Lakes Publishing, 1991.

Holland Land Company Project: Fredonia, NY: SUNY Reed Library. http://sunysb.edu/libmap/westerny.htm, May 20, 2006.

Holland Land Company Records 1801–1884: A Guide to the Microfilm Edition: Westfield, NY: Patton Library, 1992.

Holmes, Frank R., comp. *Directory of the Ancestral Heads of New England Families 1620–1700*. Baltimore: Genealogical Publishing Co., 1964.

How to Read a Two Hundred-Year-Old Document. earlyamerica. com/howto.html, May 20, 2006.

Hoyt, Edward A., ed. *State Papers of Vermont, Volume VIII, General Petitions 1778–1787.* Montpelier: Secretary of State, 1952.

Hutchins, Catherine E., ed. *Everyday Life in the Early Republic.* Winterthur, DE: H. F. du Pont Winterthur Museum, 1994.

Index of Awards on the Claims of the Soldiers of the War of 1812. Albany, NY: Weed, Parsons and Co., 1860.

Jenks, Mabel Furner. *Lima 1788–1964, Outline of the History of Lima Written for the 175th Anniversary Celebration.* Saugerties, NY: Hope Farm Press, 1964.

Jones, Henry Z Jr. *Psychic Roots: Serendipity & Intuition in Genealogy.* Baltimore: Genealogical Publishing Co., 1993.

———. *More Psychic Roots: Further Adventures in Serendipity & Intuition in Genealogy.* Baltimore: Genealogical Publishing Co., 1997.

Jones, Matt Bushell. *Vermont in the Making 1750–1779.* Hamden, CT: Archon Books, 1968.

Knights, Edwin M. Jr. "In Pursuit of Your Medical Pedigree," *Family Chronicles* (September–October 1999).

Linchlaen, John, agent of the Holland Land Company. *Journal: Travels in the Years 1791 and 1792 in Pennsylvania, New York and Vermont.* New York: G. P. Putnam and Sons; The Knickerbocker Press, 1897.

Livsey, Karen E. *Western New York Land Transactions, 1804–1824: Extracted from the Archives of the Holland Land Company.* Baltimore: Genealogical Publishing Co., 1991.

Ludlum, David M. *Social Ferment in Vermont: 1791–1850.* New York: AMS Press, Inc., 1966.

————. *Vermont Weather Book.* Montpelier: Vermont Historical Society, 1985.

McGurty, Michael S. "Congress Would Not Meet Without a Victory to Announce Them": The American Invasion of Canada in 1812." Unpublished paper, October 2003.

Middlebury (VT) Mercury, January 28, 1803, p. 1.

Middletown (VT) Baptist Church Records, 1784–1931: The Baptist Church of Middletown (1784–1931; MSA 195: 1, Records, vol. 2, 1790–1811). Montpelier: Vermont Historical Society.

Middletown Springs, Rutland County, Vermont Land Records, 1782–1880. Montpelier: Genealogical Society of Utah, 1952.

Military Papers Accounts and Muster Rolls, vol. 1, 1740–1763. Providence: Rhode Island Archives.

Nye, Mary Green, ed. *State Papers of Vermont, vol. V, Petitions for Grants of Land 1778–1811.* Montpelier: Secretary of State, 1939.

————. *State Papers of Vermont, vol. VI, Sequestration, Confiscation and Sales of Estates.* Montpelier: Secretary of State, 1941.

————. *State Papers of Vermont, vol. VII, New York Land Patents 1688–1786 covering land now included in the state of Vermont (not including Military Patents).* Montpelier: Secretary of State, 1947.

Orwell, Addison County, Vermont Land Records 1784–1887. Montpelier: Genealogical Society of Utah, 1952.

Orwell Baptist Church Minutes 1787–1805. Orwell, VT: Town Clerk's Office (Connie Hotits, clerk), 1992.

Perkins, Nathan. *A Narrative of a Tour Through the State of Vermont from April 27 to June 12, 1789 by the Rev'd*

Nathan Perkins of Hartford. Woodstock, VT: The Yankee Bookshop, 1937.

Petersen, James E. *Otter Creek: The Indian Road.* Salisbury, VT: Dunmore House, 1990.

Pierce, Frederick Clifton. *Foster Genealogy: Being the Record of the Posterity of Reginald Foster.* Chicago: Author (Press of W. B. Conkey Co.), 1899.

Potter, David E. *Early Land Grants & Title Controversy Clarendon Vermont 1761–1976.* Rutland, VT: Academy Books, 2nd printing, 1982.

Rhode Island in the Colonial wars: A List of Rhode Island Soldiers and Sailors in the Old French & Indian War 1755–1760. Providence: Rhode Island Historical Society, MCMX-Vlll.

Rising, Marsha Hoffman. *Vermont Newspaper Abstracts: 1783–1816.* Boston: New England Historic Genealogical Society, 2001.

Russell, Howard S. *A Long, Deep Furrow: Three Centuries of Farming in New England* (abridged and with a foreword by Mark Lapping). Hanover and London: University Press of New England, 1982.

Schutz, John A. *Legislators of the Massachusetts General Court 1671–1780: A Biographical Dictionary.* Boston: Northeastern University Press, 1997.

Shaw, Kenneth B. *Broadalbin Then and Now: A Pictorial History.* Broadalbin, NY: K.B.S., 1973.

Siebert, Wilbur H. *Vermont's Anti-Slavery and Underground Railroad Record.* Columbus, OH: Spahr & Glenn Co., 1937.

Simonds, Grace. *A Complete Listing of the Stones in the Whiting Cemetery in Whiting, Vermont.* Whiting: Town Clerk, 2000.

————. *Whiting's Early Town Genealogy.* Whiting: Town Clerk, 2005.

Smith, H. P., ed. *History of Addison County Vermont, With Illustrations and Biographical Sketches of Some of Its Prominent Men and Pioneers.* Syracuse, NY: D. Mason & Co., 1886.

Smith, H. P., and W. S. Rann, eds. *History of Rutland County Vermont, 1886.* Syracuse, NY: D. Mason & Co., 1886.

Stattler, Rick, processed by. *John Henry Lydius Papers.* Providence: Rhode Island Historical Society, Manuscripts Department, 2000.

Stillwell, Lewis D. *Migration from Vermont (1776–1860).* Montpelier: Vermont Historical Society, 1948.

Stryker-Rodda, Harriet. *Understanding Colonial Handwriting.* Baltimore: Genealogical Publishing Co., 1986.

Swan, Marvel G., and Donald P., comps. *Early Families of Rutland, Vermont.* Rutland: Rutland Vermont Historical Society, 1990.

Thorn, Stephen, ed. *Haswell's Vermont Almanac for the Year of our Lord 1792.* Bennington: Anthony Haswell, 1792.

Tunis, Edwin. *Colonial Craftsmen and the Beginnings of American Industry.* New York: Crowell, 1965.

Turner, Chipman P. *The Pioneer Period of Western New York.* Buffalo: Bigelow Brothers Printers, 1888.

Turner, O. *Pioneer History of Holland Purchase of Western New York.* Buffalo: Jewett, Thomas & Co., Geo. H. Derby Co, 1849, vol. 1 and 2; reprinted by James Brunner, Geneseo, 1974, vol. 15.

Ulrich, Laurel Thatcher. *A Midwife's Tale: The Life of Martha Ballard Based on Her Diary 1785–1812.* New York: Vintage Books, 1991.

United States Census Office. *1st census 1790 Heads of Families at the first census of the United States, taken in the year 1790, Vermont (1791).* Baltimore: Genealogical Publishing Co., 1975. Reprint; originally published Washington, DC: Government Printing Office, 1907.

————. *2nd census 1800 Heads of Families at the second census of the United States, taken in the year 1800, Vermont.* Baltimore: Genealogical Publishing Company, 1972. Reprint; originally published Montpelier: Vermont Historical Society, 1938.

————. *3rd Census 1810. Population Schedules of the third census of the United States 1810.* Washington, DC: National Archives, 1958–1961, National Archives microfilm publications: micro copy 252.

————. *4th census 1820 Census Schedules 1820.* Washington, DC: National Archives, 1949, 1858–60, National Archives microfilm publications: M33.

Van Camp, Julie Foster. "Ichabod's Diary: A Window to His World." *Ancestry,* vol. 18, no. 2 (March–April 2000).

Vermont, Independence and Statehood, Microsoft Encarta Encyclopedia. Microsoft Corporation: 1993–1997.

Vital Records of Attleborough, MA to 1849. Salem, MA: Essex Institute, 1934.

Waldman, Carl. *Atlas of North American Indians,* rev. ed. New York: Checkmark Books, 2000.

Webster, Elder S., and Abner Ames. *A Book of Records for the Baptist Church of Christ in Orwell, Vermont.* Orwell: 1800.

Webster, Harold and Elizabeth. *Our Whiting: Story of a Small Vermont Town.* Rutland: Academy Books, 1976.

Weissend, Patrick R. *The Life and Times of Joseph Ellicott.* http://www. hollandlandoffice.com, May 6, 2006.

Weller, Ethelyn. *North Collins and Vicinity, 1941.* http://www.buffnet.net/~macdowel/cross/georg.htm., May 20, 2006.

White, Dorothy Higson, comp. *Descendants of Roger Williams, Book III: The Sayles Line Through His Daughter Mary Williams.* Publication sponsored by Roger Williams Family Association, gift to the Rhode Island Historical Society Library, November 7, 2002.

White, Virgil. *Index of War of 1812 Pension Files*, vol. A–F. Waynesboro: National Historical Publishing Co., 1989.

Whiting, Vermont, Land Deeds, Book 3.

Wilgus, William J. *Transportation in the Development of Vermont.* Montpelier: Vermont Historical Society, 1945.

Wilson, Harold. *The Hill Country of Northern New England.* New York: Columbia University Press, 1936.

Wood, Gordon S., reviewer. *Iron Tears: America's Battle for Freedom, Britain's Quagmire: 1775–1783* by Stanley Weintraub. *New York Review of Books*, vol. 52, no. 7, April 18, 2005.

Wright, Louis B. *Everyday Life in Colonial America.* New York: Putnam, 1966.

Wright, Merideth. *Everyday Dress of Rural America 1783–1800.* New York: Dover Publications, 1990.

Julie Foster Van Camp was born and raised in Cedar Rapids, Iowa, the daughter of a Washington County farm boy turned pediatrician. She has a BA in journalism from the University of Iowa and an MS in criminal justice from Northeastern University in Boston. Her articles have appeared in *Ancestry, Western New York Heritage, New England An-*

photo by Greg Ewert

cestors, The Christian Science Monitor, The San Francisco Examiner, The Judges Journal, and various American Bar Association publications. Her books include <u>*Courts and the Classroom*</u> (Supreme Judicial Court of Massachusetts, Boston, MA) and <u>*State Courts and Law-Related Education*</u> (Phi Alpha Delta Law Fraternity, Washington, DC). After retiring in 1992, she moved to Lopez Island, Washington, where she writes and volunteers as a nonprofit management consultant.

Note: In November 2008, the property owner granted permission to dig for Ichabod's bones. Since the stones on Lot 51 do not represent a designated grave, no official state permission is required. The dig will commence in the spring of 2009, when the snow has melted. For those interested in following this continuing search for Ichabod, contact the author with the subject line Ichabod's Grave at www.searchingforichabod.com

2654965